Death of a Songbird

CHRIS GOFF

For Wes, my best friend

CONTENTS

Introduction

I had some birding experience under my belt by the time I wrote the second in the Birdwatcher's Mystery series, Death of a Songbird. This meant I could identify 161 Colorado birds, many of which visited my feeders. I had attended several more birding conventions, spent a few more days in the field and voraciously read everything that crossed my path on birding and birding issues. Weighing everything from natural predators to commercial industry impacts, I'd come to the conclusion that the biggest danger to birds were humans.

Shortly after the publication of my first book, A Rant of Ravens (centered on the illegal trading of peregrine falcons), the peregrine was delisted. This meant, it was no longer considered an endangered bird and many of the protections were lifted. Rather than face the same issue by choosing another individual bird, in Death of a Songbird I chose to focus on the coffee industry and its effects on migratory songbirds. The coffee industry is huge. It's a $20B exporting business. Worldwide coffee drinkers consume approximately 500 billion cups of coffee a year—much of it raised in full sun, requiring use of dangerous pesticides, and with notoriously underpaid workers.

In Death of a Songbird, the protagonist is EPOCH member Lark Drummond, a silent partner in a coffee house that imports fair trade, organic coffee. Early on in the story, she witnesses the murder of her partner and inherits the coffee business—along with the reason her partner was killed.

In keeping with the trend set by my first book, by the time Death of a Songbird was published, the company on which I had based Lark's company was in trouble. The owner had gone to Mexico to purchase fair trade, organic coffee and run afoul of the Chiapas Indians and the authorities. He was ultimately expelled from Mexico and banned from returning for three years.

I was now two-for-two.

Chapter 1

Coffee is to the weary what good maid service is to a luxury hotel: a necessity. Lark Drummond had neither.

She'd spent her morning as any other responsible hotel proprietor who had two maids out with the summer flu would : she'd scrubbed toilets, stripped sheets, and made beds until her back ached.

The good news was the Drummond Hotel was fully occupied. Every suite of the 132-room resort had been booked, courtesy of the Migration Alliance convention scheduled to start in Elk Park the next day. The bad news was there was no coffee and no cure for the flu in sight.

Lark tipped the coffee bag on end and watched a lone bean skitter across the Formica countertop. Outside her window and across the parking lot, the back door to the Drummond kitchen stood ajar. Only one thing blocked her dash for the pantry: Stephen Velof, the Drummond's manager.

She had snagged Velof by picture and résumé, and he'd turned out to be more photogenic than personable. What came across as handsome in pictures came off stiff and rigid in person. The staff abhorred him, the guests tolerated him. But he was good at his job, and Lark depended on his expertise.

A graduate of the University of Colorado's College of Business and Administration, Velof had majored in tourism and recreation. He'd obtained a master's degree and worked at resort hotels in Florida, Mexico, and Hawaii. Before coming to the Drummond, he'd served as assistant manager at the Broadmoor Hotel in Colorado Springs. Lark could hardly believe her luck when he'd responded to the ad she'd placed in Small Business Opportunity magazine. Needing professional help, she'd hired him on the spot. Still, the next time she hired a manager, she would insist on a face-to-face interview.

She watched as her employee threaded his way through the cars toward the carriage house, his freshly creased trousers cracking with every bend of his knees. His yellow power tie matched his personality, and his blond hair rose in small, fashionable spikes. The man oozed perfection, from his gelled hair to his tasseled loafers. No doubt, he bore news of the next crisis du jour.

So why didn't he just deal with it? Wasn't that why she paid him the big bucks?

Lark glanced at her watch. She'd agreed to meet Rachel Stanhope at the Warbler Café at one o'clock, a half hour from now. She intended to be on time.

"Good, you're still here," Velof declared through the screen. "We have another problem."

"What now?" It was a known fact that Velof considered burned toast a crisis, though she had to admit, the maid situation had been a doozie.

"The kitchen's nearly out of coffee."

That figured. Lark crumpled the empty coffee bag in her hand and pitched it toward the trash can. The wad of paper ricocheted around the rim, landing on the faded linoleum floor.

"I don't think you grasp the urgency of the situation," snapped Velof. "If you did, you wouldn't be playing basketball."

"Urgency? There is no urgency, Stephen. Only annoyance." Lark buttoned a flannel shirt over her lemon-yellow tee. "This is Wednesday. We have a coffee shipment due this afternoon."

"That's the problem." He swung the screen door open and strode into her kitchen, stooping to pick up the trash. "Chipe Coffee Company just canceled the delivery. Apparently, Esther Mills called late yesterday and left a message with the front desk."

Lark frowned. That didn't sound like Esther. "Did she say why?" Lark plopped down in a chair and tugged on a white anklet. "Or, better yet, did she say when they planned to reschedule the shipment?"

Velof consulted a pink message slip. "The clerk wrote, and I quote, 'Esther Mills called and said there will be no more coffee deliveries until further notice.'"

"That can't be right." Lark wiggled her fingers, gesturing for him to hand her the note. "Who took the message?"

"Peter Jacobs, the night clerk," Velof said, handing over the pink slip. "He's a reliable sort."

Stephen was right. Jacobs wasn't the careless type.

"Lark, I know Esther Mills is your friend, but…" Velof shook his head. "Look, I tried calling her myself. She wouldn't take my call. Frankly, if she won't or can't give us a definite delivery time, then I think we have to find another distributor."

Under normal circumstances, Lark would have agreed or at least conceded he had a point. However, Lark wasn't just Esther Mills's friend. She was Esther's business partner, albeit a silent one.

Lark handed back the message. "Before we make any rash decisions, let me check into it."

"In the best interest of the Drummond, I really must insist—"

"I said I'll do some checking." Lark pulled on her other sock and jammed her foot into a hiking boot. Velof's manner and his inferred criticism of her management style raised Lark's hackles. He seemed to forget or chose to ignore the fact that the Drummond was owner-operated, and that she, not he, was the owner.

On the other hand, Esther did owe them an explanation.

Lark yanked up on her bootlaces.

Canceled coffee deliveries were bad for business.

Yank.

Esther was nothing if not a consummate businesswoman.

Yank.

Lark remembered their first meeting, several years ago, at an evening program of the Elk Park Ornithological Chapter EPOCH presented a slide show on the birds of Rocky Mountain National Park, and Esther introduced her new "bird-supportive" coffeehouse, the Warbler Café, by distributing checklists of the bird species seen from the back deck. Two years later, when launching the Chipe Coffee Company, she'd shown up at the Elk Park Chamber of Commerce's annual luncheon toting miniature cardboard birdhouses stuffed full of gourmet coffee beans.

In need of investors, she'd explained how the Chipe Coffee Company was an organic coffee distributorship set up to supply gourmet beans up and down the Front Range. The coffee—purchased directly from Mexican growers—was pesticide-free and "bird-supportive," hence the name Chipe, pronounced cheap-ã, the Mexican word for warbler. Lark and several EPOCH members had ponied up. Anything for the birds.

So why had Esther canceled the order? Not enough supply and too much demand?

Lark gingerly wiggled her right foot into her other boot. Earlier that summer, she'd broken her ankle. Now she babied it, more out of habit than necessity. "Why wasn't the message delivered earlier?"

"I can't say," Velof answered, whining through his nose. "I only learned of it ten minutes ago, myself. It's not like I haven't been busy this morning."

"Of course." Though, who was the one up to her elbows in Tidy Bowl? Lark finished tying her boots. "I'll talk to Esther and get the skinny. I'm sure it's just some sort of mix-up."

Standing, she grabbed her scope and backpack from their ready position beside the refrigerator. Velof stiffened. "May I ask where you're going?"

"To the Warbler."

"With your birdwatching paraphernalia?"

Lark patted the backpack and hoisted it over her shoulder. "Yep."

Inside were all of her birding essentials: a pair of binoculars, a field guide, small notebook, water bottle, granola bar, pencils, lip stuff, matches, pocket knife, and sunscreen. The scope came attached to a tripod, so that she carried by hand.

"You can't just leave. That's…irresponsible."

"How so? There's not much I can do here, Stephen. One of us needs to talk to Esther, and she's at the Warbler." Lark touched his sleeve. "I promise, I'll be back in a few hours."

"In the meantime, what am I supposed to do when our guests request afternoon coffee service?"

"Serve them coffee." Lark scrambled down the porch steps, turning back at the stoop. "I'll get some answers. Meanwhile, send someone down to the grocery store and have them buy some beans."

The Warbler Café sat on the corner of Highway 34 and Village Circle, across the road from Elk Lake. The store occupied the end space of an L-shaped strip mall that squatted a half mile downhill from the Drummond. A large hand-painted mural adorned the coffee shop's front door, depicting a colorful array of Colorado's most common warblers—the yellow, yellow-rumped, Virginia's, McGillivray's, Wilson's, black-throated gray, orange-crowned, and common yellowthroat—along with the yellow-breasted chat. A narrow redwood deck wrapped the end of the building, adding a skirted effect and a place to catch the view. This afternoon, people in shorts and T-shirts crammed the railings.

Across the highway, Elk Lake shimmered serenely in the Colorado sunshine. To the north, the Drummond Hotel crowned the hillside, and to the southwest, Longs Peak towered majestically over downtown Elk Park.

Inside the café, the noise was deafening. Customers filled the tables that cluttered the hardwood floor, making navigation nearly impossible. Behind the counter, coffee machines clanged and whirred and processed. In the corner, a copper roasting machine agitated green beans and spewed the sharp scent of Mexican Jaltengo into the air.

"Lark. Over here."

Lark turned toward the voice. Rachel Stanhope waved her arms from the back of the store. Tall and willowy, with a smattering of freckles capping her nose, she looked more eighteen than thirty. Her auburn hair was pulled into a ponytail through the back of a designer baseball cap, and she wore a pink crop top emblazoned with DKNY over tight-fitting jeans.

Lark fingered her braid and glanced down at her own attire. Flannel shirt. Dusty shorts. A definite thirty, going on thirty-five. While Rachel looked like a redheaded Jennifer Aniston, Lark looked like Heidi, back from a week with the goats.

Plowing her way to the table, Lark dumped her backpack and scope in one of the vacant chairs. "Man, this place is a zoo. Have you ordered yet?"

Rachel shook her head. "I waited for you. I wasn't sure if you

6

wanted to stay or take something to go."

"I'd say go, except that I need to talk to Esther."

"I'm not sure she's here," Rachel said. "I haven't seen her, but here comes Teresa. She'll know where she is."

Teresa Cruz was the eighteen-year-old daughter of one of the Chipe Coffee Company's Mexican coffee growers, and another of Esther's projects. According to Esther, Teresa had fallen in love with a young man whom her father considered unsuitable. He'd retaliated by sending her stateside.

"Hola," said Teresa. Her low, husky voice, laced with a thick Mexican accent, sounded odd coming from someone so small. A little over five feet tall, she had a flat nose, wide lips, and wore her long, dark hair knotted loosely at her nape. Dressed in blue jeans and tennis shoes, she looked like any American teenager. A white Indian peasant blouse brought out her deep mahogany coloring. "What can I get for you?"

"Something tall and strong," replied Lark, smiling at the girl. "Do you know where Esther is?"

"No," snapped Teresa.

Lark and Rachel glanced at each other.

Teresa jerked her head in the direction of the counter. "Maybe she's in the back. Maybe not." Teresa poked the end of her pencil toward Rachel. "What do you want?"

"The same as Lark."

"Two double espressos." Teresa scribbled the order on a pad, then rubbed her temple with the pencil's eraser. "Do you want cream?"

Lark and Rachel both nodded.

"Got it. Con crema. I'll be back."

"Hold on," Lark said.

Teresa hesitated. "What?"

"Will you do me a favor?"

"Maybe."

"Tell Esther I need to talk to her."

"If I can find her." Teresa shrugged a shoulder, then turned and wiggled her way through the crowd.

"What's her problem?" Lark queried, staring after the girl, amazed at how quickly she moved without seeming to hurry.

7

Halfway to the counter, Teresa froze, then abruptly changed course and hurried away in a different direction.

"Don't know. Maybe she's tired?" Rachel offered. "Have you ever seen it this packed in here? This is absurd."

Lark allowed her gaze to sweep the crowd. There did seem to be a lot of tourists in town. Last year, Elk Park had hosted over three million visitors: old people, young people, families, people of all nationalities. They thronged to "the gateway to Rocky Mountain National Park," and a fair percentage drank coffee at the Warbler. But for late August, this crowd was heavy.

"A lot of these people must be here for the Migration Alliance convention," Lark said. The MA was a co-op of government agencies, organizations, and individuals banded together by issues involving migratory birds and their habitats. Every summer, their annual convention drew over twelve hundred participants. Much to Lark's satisfaction, they'd designated Elk Park as this year's site.

"Do you see anyone you know?"

"Paul Owens is sitting over there." Lark leaned in closer and pointed. "Do you see the guy with the tall blond woman? They're sitting at a table near the counter, two tables this side of the cash register."

"You mean the guy who looks like Robert Redford?"

Lark cocked her head and squinted. "Which movie?"

"Butch Cassidy and the Sundance Kid"

Lark studied Owens for a moment. Medium height, blond hair, and bad skin, hard to see at a distance yet noticeable. "He does sort of resemble Bob, doesn't he?"

Rachel nodded. "So why should I recognize his name?"

"Paul Owens is MA's new executive director. He sets the Alliance agenda. He decides which projects get attention, which ones flounder, that sort of thing. In other words, he has all the power, and he wields it with a deft hand."

"What you're saying is, he's the boss, and he knows it."

Lark grinned. "Something like that."

Teresa reappeared and deposited two steaming cups of espresso on the table. "Dos. To go. Sorry, but we're all out of glasses. You need anything more?"

"Just the check." Lark dug in her pocket for money.

"Gracias." Teresa ripped the top sheet off her notepad, slapped it down on the table, and waited for Lark to pay. "By the way, Esther told me to tell you that she doesn't have time for talking right now. She wants to know if you can come back after the rush."

Lark frowned. Based on the number of customers, Esther's request seemed reasonable. But when it came to issues involving the Drummond, Lark liked things resolved.

"Hey, don't look mad at me. I'm just the delivery boy."

"Girl," Lark corrected. "Delivery girl." She handed Teresa a ten. "Keep the change." Then, forcing a smile, she jerked her head toward the coffee bar. "Tell Esther I'll be back."

"Did I miss something?" Rachel asked, after Teresa had stepped away. "Is there something going on between you and Esther?"

"Nope," Lark said, snatching up her scope and backpack. "Not a thing."

"Right, which is why you're practically fuming."

"I am not fuming." Lark rolled the tension from her shoulders. She was concerned, not angry. And she wanted to know why Esther was avoiding her.

"You could have fooled me."

"Look, it's nothing," Lark said, as much in an attempt to convince herself as to convince Rachel. "Esther canceled the Drummond coffee shipment last night and never rescheduled it. That's all. I just need to know when to expect it."

"Right." Rachel looked skeptical.

"It's just…Don't you get the feeling Esther's avoiding me? I mean…" Lark held up her thumb. "First she cancels the Drummond's coffee delivery without rescheduling." Another finger went up. "Then she refuses to take Stephen's phone call. Now she claims she doesn't have time to talk."

"Well…she's busy," Rachel said, gesturing at the crowd. "Besides, you're talking about one canceled order."

"Easy for you to say. You're not the one trying to run a business." Lark snatched up her espresso, sloshing coffee over

9

the sides of the cup. Grabbing up a napkin, she blotted up the mess, then moved toward the exit before Rachel could respond.

It wasn't so much the cancellation that bothered her, Lark realized. It was the other things. Of all the EPOCH members investing in the Chipe Coffee Company, Lark had been the most enthusiastic. She'd pitched in to the tune of two hundred fifty thousand dollars, knowing full well the first three years of a new operation were the most critical. She'd signed the general partnership agreement with her eyes wide open, knowing her total investment was at risk. And she'd even agreed to take a silent role in the business. The bottom line was, she had a lot riding on Esther's business acumen.

And up to now, she had no reason to doubt it, she reminded herself. Truth be told, the Chipe Coffee Company was doing remarkably well.

A resounding crash cut her thoughts short and brought her to a halt two feet from the front door.

The room fell dead silent.

Behind the counter, Esther and Teresa stood nose to nose, equal in stature, their eyes locked, their faces flushed. One fair, one dark. One middle-aged, one young. One angry, one scared.

"Why you stupid, stupid little—"

"Don't call me names!" Teresa's hair had come loose, and she swept it away from her face with a flourish before jutting a finger at Esther. "I've worked hard for you. And for what, huh? For the measly minimum wage? You promised me the money."

"I don't have it." Esther retreated a step. "Besides, after what's happened, you're crazy to think that you'll ever see another penny out of me."

"But you owe it to me. It's mine."

Esther drew herself up, squaring thin shoulders. "I don't owe you a damn thing. The truth is, I'm sending you home."

Teresa's face blanched.

"I have already called your father."

"You can't do this."

Esther's lips curled in a tight smile. "Sure I can."

Teresa's gaze flitted over the riveted crowd, darting from face to face. "Please, Señora Mills, don't send me back there."

10

"The fact is, Teresa, I've booked a reservation on the next plane. You leave for Chiapas first thing tomorrow morning."

Teresa balled her hands into fists. "I won't go. You can't make me leave." Her eyes glistened. "I won't let you send me back there."

Esther crossed her arms. "And pray tell, how do you intend to stop me?"

Teresa's chin quivered, then her face hardened into an angry mask. "I will do whatever I must."

Chapter 2

The declaration hung in the air. Time and movement froze, then Teresa, red-faced and trembling, slammed out the back door and disappeared.

Esther puffed out a breath, turning to the startled patrons. "Everyone, go back to your coffee," she said, wafting her hands through the air as though clearing a foul smell. "I apologize for any disturbance. Please, everything's fine now." Her blue gaze lighted on Lark. "There's nothing to worry about. Really."

Lark's stomach muscles tightened. She wished she believed her.

Turning away, Esther rang up orders at the cash register, her fingers alternating between punching in numbers and tucking errant strands of tinted blond hair behind her ears. Between smiles, her teeth worked at peeling layers of skin from her lower lip. And every so often, she glanced nervously over her shoulder.

"Now I'm sure something odd is going on," declared Rachel, jarring Lark from her trancelike observation.

Lark didn't respond. Instead, she pushed through the front door in time to see Teresa speed away in a dented Volkswagen. The car, a two-toned bug complete with mag wheels and a sunroof, belonged to Esther. It was a relic from bygone days – passed down to a younger generation. The type of car that required contortionist moves to make out in the backseat. The type daddies loved to give to their little girls.

"I wonder what that was all about?" Rachel asked. She had trailed after Lark into the parking lot and stood with her hands shoved deep into her back pockets.

"I haven't a clue." Lark watched the bug skid around the corner, amazed it remained on all four wheels. "Do you consider that car theft?"

"Esther might."

Lark nodded. Esther would. Lark shouldered her backpack and scope. "Ready?"

"You mean we're still going?" Rachel slipped her hands free.

"I assumed the birdwatching was canceled. I figured you would want to stick around and talk to Esther."

Rae had pegged that right, thought Lark, but she didn't see the point in sticking around. There were too many people inside the store right now to carry on a private conversation, and business woes weren't something she wanted to publicize. "I'll stick with the game plan and catch her at closing."

"Great, then I'll grab my things." Rachel crossed the parking lot and retrieved a leather backpack from her aunt's green Toyota. She paused before shutting the door. "Do you want to drive over?"

Lark shook her head. "We're just crossing the street."

"I know, but…" Rachel's gaze darted to Lark's ankle.

Two months ago, Lark had broken it taking a header off a cliff on Twin Owls. Search and Rescue had been called out, and they'd hauled her fanny off the mountain on a stretcher. Not one of her better moments. "I think I can make it."

"You're sure?"

"Positive."

To make her point, Lark struck off down the deer path, ignoring the twinge of pain brought on by memory. After spending the first six weeks of the summer in a cast and the next four limping, she intended to enjoy every nanosecond left of the summer season. The fact was, the ankle only really bothered her in damp weather, and Colorado had been dry. Unusually dry.

Overhead, the sun burned brightly, emphasizing the point, igniting pangs of guilt deep in her consciousness. While Lark paid homage to the sun god, Colorado needed rain. With the snowpack long since melted, every ray of sunshine beating down escalated the drought conditions that plagued the Front Range and elevated fire danger in the high country.

"I hate to belabor a point," Rachel said, crunching behind her through the dry, brown grass. "But why are you so upset?"

"Let it go, Rae."

"No." Rachel stopped crunching. "I want to know what's bothering you."

Lark took several more strides, then turned back. "It's the fact she won't communicate."

13

Without any more prodding, she told Rachel about her first meeting with Esther, about the business idea, about the investment. "Then, for no reason, she up and cancels the coffee deliveries."

"One delivery," Rachel pointed out.

"All deliveries. Until further notice," countered Lark.

"So, let me get this straight, you and Esther are partners in the Warbler Café?"

"In the Chipe Coffee Company, to be exact." Lark moved on, scampering down the embankment that edged Highway 34. The baked earth crumbled easily beneath her feet, and she rode the rivulets to the ditch. "Chipe serves as an umbrella company," she continued, once Rachel had surfed the road cut. "The Warbler was annexed into the agreement when we formed the new partnership."

"So, are there additional investors?"

"Three. Dorothy and Cecilia, and…" Lark paused, unsure how Rachel would react to the next name. "Gertie."

Gertrude Tanager was Rachel's cousin by virtue of marriage. Her father, William, had married Rachel's aunt, Miriam. At best, the cousins tolerated each other. At worst, Gertie publicly flogged Rachel for being the niece of "a gold digger," while Rachel dismissed Gertie as being crass and unimaginative.

"You're not serious?" Rachel exclaimed.

"Deadly." Lark inched her way along the shoulder, waiting for a break in the traffic. "Personally, I never thought she'd come up with the cash."

That had surprised all of them, except perhaps Esther. But then, she didn't know Gertie like the rest of them did. Gertie was the type who asked you to lunch, ordered the most expensive item on the menu, then never had any money when it came time to pay the bill. By Lark's guess, Gertie banked on her inheritance in order to raise the needed capital.

On the other hand, Dorothy and Cecilia had money to burn. Besides being well-heeled by birth, both sisters received a monthly pension—Dorothy MacBean as a retired schoolteacher, and Cecilia Meyer as an army widow.

"How much money did Gertie invest?"

Lark, having been raised to believe it was in bad taste to discuss one's—anyone's—finances, skirted Rachel's question. "The start-up costs totaled six hundred fifty thousand dollars. I put up some, Esther threw in the Warbler, and the others put up a combined total of around one hundred fifty thousand dollars. Esther used the new capital to order coffee supplies, rent a warehouse, that sort of stuff."

"So exactly how much came from Gertie? Fifty thousand?"

"Does it really matter?"

Before she could answer, Lark spotted an opening in the traffic. Signaling for Rachel to follow, Lark sprinted onto the highway. Her feet slapped the pavement, then a sharp stab of pain shot up her right ankle. Her foot buckled. She lurched, then fell into the path of an oncoming Winnebago.

Lark scrambled to regain her footing. The driver braked, squealing his tires against the warm asphalt. Lark crabwalked sideways, recovered her balance, and hopped to the other side.

"Are you okay?" Rachel yelled, scooting across the road behind the motor home.

"Fine." Lark bent over and exhaled hard. "That was close."

"That's an understatement." Rachel jostled Lark's shoulder. "So, were you trying to get out of answering my question?"

Lark straightened, squinting through the bright sunshine. "About Gertie's investment?"

"Yes."

"Why is it so important?"

Lark turned and limped up the knoll, trying to convince herself the pain in her ankle would dissipate with use. They walked in silence for a moment, then Rachel asked, "How much do you know about Aunt Miriam's financial situation?"

"Practically nothing." She and Miriam were friends, not family, and separated in age by decades. "I know that after William died, Miriam inherited Bird Haven."

"That's where you're wrong. Uncle Will left his share of the estate to his three daughters. Aunt Miriam retains the right to live at Bird Haven, but only if she doesn't remarry or sell any portion of the ranch. Any deviation from the terms, and she's forced to sell out to pay off the Tanager sisters."

That explained some of the animosity between Gertie and Rachel, thought Lark. And between Gertie and her stepmother. "What does any of that have to do with Gertie's investment in Chipe Coffee?"

"The sisters claim they need the money from Uncle William's estate. They've asked Aunt Miriam to sell Bird Haven. She refused, of course, so now the girls are threatening to petition her through the courts. What I want to know is, if they're all so strapped for funds, where did Gertie get the money to invest?"

"Good question."

Lark thought for a moment. Gertie worked at the bank. She might have taken out a loan. Or maybe the sisters weren't as strapped for funds as they wanted Miriam to believe they were. If that were the case, in spite of a possible legal obligation to keep the terms of the partnership agreement confidential, friendship overrode rules. "Gertie put up fifty thousand."

"Dollars?"

"As in U.S. currency. We put up the cash; Esther runs the show."

"Surely you have a say in how things operate?"

"None. Zip. As in, we don't speak unless spoken to."

"Even you? Didn't you say you put up the bulk of the money?"

"Yeah, but it was part of the arrangement."

"And you don't have a problem with that?"

"I didn't until today. I considered the business an investment, and with Esther at the helm, I knew I'd see a return on my money. Heck, Esther drew cash out of the Warbler Café the first year she opened it."

"That's pretty good."

"That's darn good. It usually takes a new business three years to turn profit. Anyway, after seeing how well she did with the café, I figured I could trust her. At least, until she canceled our coffee and made no attempt at rebooking the delivery." Lark stopped at the top of the knoll and sat down to rest her ankle in the short grass along the golf course. Gently, she massaged the sore joint, soaking in the view of the lake and golf course and gulping deep breaths of the fresh mountain air. "So tell me, Rae. Why am I making mountains out of molehills?"

Rachel tugged at a tall stalk of grass, then twisted it around her finger. "Maybe because you have a small fortune on the line?"

"Yeah, maybe." Though, in reality, Lark's fortune was tied up in the Drummond Hotel, perched majestically on the hillside behind them.

The lavish, five-story Victorian building had been built in the early 1900s by James Drummond, Lark's great-grandfather. Like others of his time, he had moved to the area for his health, fallen in love with Elk Park, and stayed. Forced to live in rustic accommodations, he'd spotted the potential for building a luxury resort hotel amidst the beautiful surroundings, and the Drummond—complete with ballroom, music room, billiard room, dining room, and bar, and adjoined by a carriage house, concert hall, eighteen-hole golf course and Manor House—opened for business in 1909. James and his wife played hosts to the rich and famous, and the Drummond Hotel had quickly flourished, becoming one of the country's most popular resort destinations. Then, in the 1920s, they sold out, vesting a large number of trust funds, several of which still lived on in perpetuity.

Not Lark's. Three years ago, she had signed hers away for ownership of the Drummond, spending all but the two hundred fifty thousand dollars she invested in the Chipe Coffee Company.

"Lark, do you think Esther's argument with Teresa had something to do with the canceled deliveries?" Rachel asked, still toying with the thin blade of grass.

"I'll admit, the thought crossed my mind. But I can't figure out how. Teresa's a waitress. I don't see that there's any way she could have affected Chipe Coffee Company's deliveries."

"Isn't her father a grower? Maybe they're holding a bean shipment hostage in exchange for Teresa's safe return to Mexico."

"The Juan Valdez coffee wars?" Lark grinned and shook her head. "Nice theory, but Teresa's father sent her here. He'd be

17

more apt to refuse to sell Esther more coffee if she sent Teresa back. You know that she buys all her coffee direct from the growers?"

Rachel shook her head.

"Well, she does. She goes to Chiapas twice a year, personally inspects all the beans, then loads them into a big rental truck and drives them home."

Rachel nibbled thoughtfully on the stem of grass. "So why do you think she's sending Teresa home? Because of something she did, or just because Esther's tired of having a houseguest?"

"Probably something she did." Then again, Esther wasn't just some middle-aged, business-oriented spinster who'd relish some company. She lived with Victor Garcia, the Elk Park County sheriff. It wasn't inconceivable that she—or Vic, for that matter—might want Teresa to leave so they could have the house back to themselves.

Nah. Given Vic's work with troubled youth and Esther's devotion to causes, it seemed highly unlikely they would just send Teresa away for no reason. Lark pushed herself up from the grass. "Let's keep going."

After brushing off her rear end, Lark set off across the golf course, joined the paved trail encircling Elk Lake, then turned onto a rough, graveled path that snaked south toward the lake. A felled log lay crosswise on the gravel, guaranteeing foot traffic only; sentinels of cottonwoods, Colorado blue spruce, and ponderosa pine stood guard at the mouth of the trail. A large sign proclaimed they were embarking upon the Paris Mills Nature Trail.

The nature trail—named after Esther Mills' grandmother, once considered one of Elk Park's leading ladies—crisscrossed a twenty-acre piece of land on the north side of the lake. Bordered on the east by water and on the west by the paved trail and golf course, the trail meandered along the edge of a small peninsula and another half-mile stretched along the lake's edge.

"Let's set up on the point," Lark suggested. "We'll get a nice view from out there and lots of waterfowl to practice on."

Rachel nodded, then pushed ahead.

For someone who'd never done much birdwatching, thought

Lark, Rae had taken to the sport like a duck to water. She'd gone from being a novice with an attitude in June to being an aficionada by mid-August. Given a few more pointers, a few more scoping lessons, and a few more books to devour, she ought to graduate to the "I know enough to be dangerous" sector by mid-September.

If she would even be around that long. Miriam was due back from her birding trip to the Middle East in a couple of weeks; Rachel planned to go back to New York after her return. Lark would be sorry to see her go.

"How about setting up here?" Rachel asked, pointing to a flat area with a view of the water and the Warbler Café. From this vantage point, even without a scope, Lark could easily spot several species of duck paddling the lake.

"Looks good." She swung the equipment off her shoulder, dropping the pack at the foot of a large ponderosa pine. "Now, the first thing we have to do is set up and adjust the tripod." Extending the tripod's legs, she pointed to the liquid bubble. "Mine has a leveling device, so perfection becomes an option, if you're into that. All I care about is close and comfortable. Eyepiece height is the most important thing."

Since they were both using her setup, Lark adjusted the height slightly higher than usual, then pointed out the scope's features: the eighty-millimeter lens, the fifteen to forty-five-power zoom eyepiece. "I like the angled eyepiece, because I don't have to crane my neck as much. Just look down into it."

"What's this?" Rachel asked, pointing to a bright pink cap at the end of the scope.

"The bottom of a large plastic yogurt container." Lark pulled it off and stuffed the makeshift lens cap into her backpack, where it wouldn't get dusty. Next she focused on a large mallard drake, then stepped aside to give Rachel a look. "Do you see how clearly he comes in? Now try zooming the eyepiece."

Rachel practiced focusing and zooming for a while, then Lark showed her how to pan by releasing the tripod lock and swiveling the scope.

"Oh, look, there's one with a moon on its face," Rachel said. She fiddled with the eyepiece.

"Crescent-shaped?"

"Here, you look."

Lark ducked her head and peered through the eyepiece. The duck, brownish gray and mottled, had a black tail and a prominent white crescent behind its bill. "It's called a blue-winged teal."

Rachel stretched to look again. "I don't see any blue."

"Trust me, it's there. The duck has a powder-blue wing patch. Sometimes it's hard to see, unless the bird's flying. Then you can't miss it."

Lark kept a list of the ducks they identified: the mallard, the blue-winged teal, the ring-necked duck, and the common merganser. Then she challenged Rachel to try and get close-ups of the bird species in the trees.

The afternoon drifted lazily. Squirrels chattered in the pines, answered occasionally by the scolding call of a raven. Violet-green swallows and tree swallows darted in and out of the branches overhead. A yellow warbler flitted from willow to birch. Lark dozed with her back propped against the warm bark of a tall ponderosa.

"This one's different."

Rachel's excitement-tinged voice yanked Lark from dreams of Tidy Bowl and sparkling toilets, and she rubbed her eyes. "Describe it."

"It has a red head."

Reluctantly, Lark pushed up from her seat under the pine. "And?"

The lens pointed across the water toward the aspens and pine rimming the north side of the lake. Using her naked eye, she spotted from the end of the scope, catching a glimpse of red and yellow in the branches. A western tanager? "I saw the red. Does it have a yellow body, with black wings and a black tail?"

"No. It's more gray, with a black headband."

"Let me look," Lark said, pushing Rachel aside.

Rachel rubbed her shoulder. "It's dead center."

While Lark refocused, the bird took flight Darn. "Do you see it, Rae? Where did it go?"

Rachel pointed left. "There. Up in the tree."

"Which tree?" There were hundreds to choose from. Lark panned the scope, zooming in on the bird as it perched on a small limb. Excitement hummed through her veins. She'd never seen a bird like this one before. "Can you find my notebook and pen?"

"Where are they?"

"Try in my backpack." Lark heard Rachel rummaging in the pack and resisted hurrying her. "Did you find them?"

"Got 'em."

"Take notes," Lark ordered. "The bird is warbler-sized, with a red face, throat, and chest. It has a black cap that extends down its neck, with gray wings, back, and tail. Its underparts look white, and it has a white patch on the back of its neck."

The bird flew again.

"Shoot," Lark said, swinging the scope left. Too far left! The parking lot behind the Warbler Café loomed into view.

In the lens, a black-hooded figure raised an arm. Sunlight glinted off something silver.

Blinded, Lark swung the scope right in search of the bird. In her mind's eye, the glint of silver coalesced into a knife. Breathing hard, she jerked the scope back left.

"What are you doing?" Rachel asked, pointing in the opposite direction. "The bird's over there."

Lark squinted through the lens. The arm dropped. Silver flashed. Esther Mills screamed in silent pain.

Chapter 3

Lark gripped the handle of the scope and zoomed the lens tighter. This time, when the black-hooded figure raised his arm, silver dripped red.

"No! Oh, no!" Lark screamed as the arm dropped again. Swallows flushed overhead, darting chaotically in flashes of white, violet green, and rust. The red-faced bird streaked away.

"What is it?" Rachel asked. "What's wrong?"

Lark's heart banged in her chest. "He's wearing a black mask with letters. E, Z, L, N. And gloves."

The figure turned. Angry eyes stared in their direction, seeming to burn across the distance, though reality said the eyes were too far away to see. The figure turned and disappeared as quickly as a startled chickadee. Lark tilted the scope down. Esther Mills's body lay in a crumpled heap on the asphalt.

"Do you have your phone?" she demanded, hoping that today wouldn't be an exception to the fact that Rachel always carried her phone.

"Why?"

Lark raised her voice. "Do you have it?"

"Yes." Rachel rooted inside her backpack. "It's here somewhere."

"Find it and call nine-one-one." Lark sprinted toward the trail, yelling at Rachel over her shoulder, "Tell them Esther Mills has just been stabbed."

"What?" Rachel cried, scrambling after her.

"Call them! I saw it happening, just now." Lark crashed through the underbrush, startling birds and squirrels, and outrunning a frightened cottontail to reach the trail. Her heart banged against her rib cage. Pain tore at her side. Rachel scrambled behind her, yelling into the phone.

It didn't take long to reach the highway, but took forever to cross. Carloads, busloads, and motor homes full of people streamed past on the four lanes, a rushing river of humanity pouring into town for the weekend. In the distance, sirens blared. Traffic slowed to a crawl.

Unable to wait any longer, Lark flung her arms above her head and stepped into the road. "Stop! Emergency! Let me pass."

Tires squealed, and a middle-aged man in a car with Texas license plates laid on his horn. The scenario played out three times, until a cowboy in a Dodge pickup read her intent and waved her through. With Rachel dogging her heels and crawling behind her up the steep embankment, Lark raced along the deer path, rounding the corner into the parking lot. When they reached the back entrance to the Warbler, Victor Garcia, the Elk Park County sheriff, was already on scene. He sat in the middle of the parking lot on the hot asphalt, cradling Esther Mills's head in his lap. Blood spread across the front of his khaki uniform, and tears streaked his face, dripping from the ends of his moustache.

"She's gone," he keened. He squeezed Esther's body tighter and buried his face in the crook of her neck. "She's dead."

Lark knew from experience that she didn't handle situations like this one well. Rachel, on the other hand, handled them like a pro. Glancing at her friend, Lark whispered, "What do we do?"

Rachel bolted into action, dropping to her knees beside Vic. "Are you positive she's dead? Did you check for a pulse?"

Lark shuddered as Rachel pressed her fingers against Esther's neck, then suppressed a scream when Vic let Esther's body fall away from his chest – Esther's lime-green shirt was torn and drenched with blood. Her throat was gashed. Her head hung limp. Half-opened eyes stared at nothing.

Lark prayed for the police to arrive. "Do you feel a pulse, Rae?"

"No. She's dead. She's definitely dead."

The sight of Rachel's fingers pressed against Esther's cooling flesh caused Lark's stomach to roil. It was time to throw up in the bushes.

Blaring sirens forced her to pull herself together, saving her from the embarrassment. Three police cars wheeled into the parking lot, officers pouring out of the doors.

Bernie Crandall, Elk Park's police chief, clambered out of the nearest cruiser and lumbered toward them. "What's going on here?"

"It's about time you showed up," Lark said.

A good old boy from the get-go, Crandall was blond and burly and possessed a boyish charm that won over the ladies and made men feel like they'd just found a new best friend. It took him less than a second to assess the situation. "Did you kill her, Garcia?"

Anger contorted Vic's features. His dark eyes narrowed into slivers of rage.

"No, he didn't," blurted Lark, turning to face Crandall, glad for an excuse not to look at Esther's body.

"How do you know, Drummond? Did you kill her?"

"No, I saw it happen." A chill scooted along Lark's spine. "I witnessed it through the scope."

Crandall arched his eyebrows and rubbed one cheek as though assessing his need for a shave. Finally, he clicked his tongue against the roof of his mouth.

"Okay, here's what we're gonna do," he said, pointing at Lark. "Drummond, I want you in my police car. Rachel, you go with Officer Klipp. Vic, you and I will take over there. You need to step away from the body."

Vic continued rocking Esther in his lap.

"Now," Crandall ordered.

Vic glanced up. He hesitated momentarily, then gently lowered Esther's body to the pavement. Stroking her hair back from her face, he mumbled something in Spanish.

"I said now." Crandall steered Vic toward the far curb, then singled out an officer to go down to the lake and collect Lark's abandoned gear. The rest of his men were given the arduous task of gathering evidence.

On the job, Crandall had a reputation for being thorough. Conscientious to the point of fastidiousness, he was a hard worker and identified well with the locals. Like most officers, he took advantage of the perks: free coffee and doughnuts at the Mountain Top Bakery, free papers at the Elk Park Gazette. But, all in all, he was the sort of cop you wanted investigating your case. A stand-up kind of guy.

Off duty was another story. On his own time, he used his position to impress the seasonal coeds, and, from what Lark could see, he rarely lacked for company. She had yet to figure out what women saw in him. To her, he looked like an aging high school football star whose muscles were turning to flab.

"If they're done with me first, I'll wait for you in the Toyota," Rachel said, passing Lark en route to Officer Klipp's car. "Otherwise, I'll leave it unlocked."

Lark nodded, then sauntered over to Bernie Crandall's cruiser. Rather than climbing inside, she leaned against the front fender, eavesdropping on his interrogation of Vic Garcia.

Technically, the Warbler Café rested inside the city limits. That put Crandall and the Elk Park Police Department in charge. But Vic Garcia had been first on the scene, and, as Elk Park County sheriff, he could commandeer jurisdiction. It wasn't likely he'd exercise the option, though. Not considering his relationship to the deceased.

"So, Vic," Crandall said in a voice designed to carry. "How'd you beat us here? I was standing in dispatch when the call came in, three minutes away."

Then why did it take you ten to get here? Lark strained to hear Vic's response. He spoke softly, his head down.

"Esther and I had a date."

"Where were you taking her?"

"Milo's."

"Fancy Italian. Flowers, wine, and romance."

Milo's required reservations. Crandall would check.

Vic crushed the palms of his hands to his eyes. "I got here too late."

Crandall laid a hand on Vic's shoulder. "God knows, this is hard, but you must've seen something."

Vic shook his head.

"Nothing? No car speeding away from the parking lot? No person fleeing the scene? I mean, you were here within minutes of the crime being committed."

"I didn't see anyone, anything." His voice broke. "Just Esther."

"Not a soul?" Crandall clucked again. "How about sounds?

Did you hear anything? Voices? Running?"

"Nothing." Vic shook his head again. "Sorry."

Crandall scratched his scalp along his part line, then stretched, cupping his hands at the back of his neck. "So, tell me something, Vic. How were you and Esther getting along?"

Vic's head snapped up. His eyes narrowed. "What kind of question is that, Bernie?"

"Just routine."

"We're getting along fine." Vic stroked his mustache, twice.

Lark noticed his use of the present tense, and she shuddered. It took time to get used to using the past tense. Maybe longer when it was someone you loved who had died. She wondered how long Vic would think of Esther as part of the present and not part of the past.

"You hadn't had any recent arguments? Any disagreements?"

"None."

It was obvious where Bernie was headed with this line of questioning. The majority of murders were committed by someone the victim knew: crimes of passion, acts of rage, committed in the heat of the moment. It was logical to suspect the boyfriend.

But Vic? He had worked in law enforcement for nearly thirty years. He was a model citizen, well-liked in the community, and he dedicated most of his spare time to working with troubled youth, a calling that by most people's estimation required infinite patience.

Lark's thoughts wandered back to the scene in the parking lot: Vic cradling Esther's body, his tears mingling with her blood. In Lark's mind's eye, she had witnessed a display of grief. Was he actually expressing remorse?

And who could hold to the "someone you know" theory? It hadn't held true seven weeks ago, when Donald Bursau, a reporter for Birds of a Feather magazine, had been found shot to death in The Thicket. While his murder might have been considered a crime of passion, Bursau barely knew his killer.

So, why else did a person murder someone?

Self-defense?

Revenge?

Power?

Greed? Money. More than likely, that was it. Just a robbery gone south.

Crandall signaled to one of his men. "Take Vic home. Keep an eye on him." He spoke softly to another officer, then swaggered across the parking lot toward the cruiser and Lark.

"Okay, tell me what you know, Drummond," he ordered, leaning against the fender beside her. By now, the warm, sunny day had faded to dusk, and Lark shivered as a cool breeze swept over the lake and up the hillside. Pink-tinged clouds crowned the mountain peaks to the west. Behind her, Esther Mills's body lay cooling on the black asphalt.

"I saw the guy stab her," she said, then filled Crandall in on the details—how she'd been teaching Rachel to use the scope, how they'd spotted an unusual bird, and how she'd happened to focus on the parking lot behind the Warbler.

"What did the perp look like?"

"I don't know. He was wearing a black ski mask."

"He?" Crandall scooted his butt onto the fender, allowing his feet to dangle by the front tire. "You're sure it was a he?"

She thought about that, trying to picture the figure in her mind. "No. I'm not sure." She pulled the braid off her neck and toyed with its end. "I guess it could have been a woman." She'd just assumed it was a man because of the brutality of the crime. "His or her ski mask covered everything. It was one of those hats with the eye holes and mouth opening."

"You say it was all black?"

"Yeah. Well, wait, not exactly all black."

Crandall pinched the bridge of his nose and exhaled loudly.

"It was mostly black. It had some lettering on it."

"What type of lettering? A logo?"

Lark shook her head. "No. I think there were four letters, but they didn't spell anything." She closed her eyes and tried re-creating the scene. She remembered the figure, the raised arm, then snapped her eyes open. "E, Z, something, something."

"Probably personal initial, or maybe some sort of organizational logo." Crandall rubbed his chin. "I thought you said you got a good look at this guy."

"A look, not a good one." Lark rubbed her forehead where a dull pain was beginning to throb. "Give me a break, Bernie. I was at least a quarter mile away."

Crandall rolled his eyes. "So how big was he?"

"Bigger than Esther." But then, who wasn't? Besides, she was cowering.

"Do you think they were close enough to the building that the guy was standing on the curb back there?"

"No, I don't think so," Lark said. "But maybe. I just don't think the angle was right for that."

Crandall drummed his hands on the fender. "So when you got up here, was Vic already holding the body?"

Lark hugged her arms around herself. An hour ago, Esther lived and breathed. Now, she was the body, the deceased. "Yeah."

Absently, Crandall swung his feet, bouncing them off the front tire of the car. "Do you remember anything else? Did you see what the suspect was wearing, besides the mask? Did he have on gloves? Any jewelry?"

"I remember he was wearing gloves." She reached up, massaging the muscles behind her ears. "Everything happened so fast. I remember seeing the guy raise his arm, a flash of silver, and then the blood."

A vision of Esther's face, her mouth opened in terror, flashed through Lark's memory as Crandall pounded a dirge on the fender. Behind them, two Elk Park PD officers stuffed Esther's body into a bag, then carried it to the coroner's station wagon. The forensic team had picked up and moved to an area near the back door of the Warbler Café.

"Did you see anyone else?" Crandall asked. "What about employees? Did you see any sign of Teresa or Scott?"

"No, only the killer and Esther." Lark turned away as the coroner slammed the station wagon's tailgate. "Besides, Teresa left early."

"How do you know?"

"I saw her leave."

"When?"

28

"About one o'clock. I was in the café with Rachel. I don't think Teresa planned to come back." Ever.

"Why? Why'd she leave?"

Lark swallowed, calming the queasiness in her stomach. The sight of the body bag and the questions about Teresa had caused Lark's stomach to roil again. She didn't know whether to barf on Bernie's shoes or answer him. Heck, he was bound to hear the story from someone eventually. "She had an argument with Esther."

Crandall cocked his eyebrows. "About what?"

"Money."

"What, she wanted a raise?"

"All I know is, she said Esther owed her some money. But she's eighteen years old. Gas money would be important to her." Lark realized she was minimizing the argument, but for some reason, she felt a need to protect Teresa, especially with Esther gone. But what if Teresa had killed her?

"Hey, Chief," called out one of the officers combing the area.

Crandall looked up. "Yo."

"Got any idea where we can find a set of keys for the store?" asked the officer, walking toward them.

"Did you check the deceased's pockets or her handbag?" Crandall jerked his head in the direction of the coroner's wagon. "Or try reaching Harvey. He owns the strip mall."

The officer flashed Crandall a thumbs-up. Crandall turned back to Lark. "I have one more question. Do you have any idea who we should notify about Esther?"

Lark stared down at her shoes. "Did you ask Vic?"

"He claims she doesn't have any next of kin. I thought, you being Esther's friend and all…well, I figured you might know if she had any business associates."

Gooseflesh prickled Lark's skin. "I'm one of her partners."

Crandall's eyes widened. "Since when?"

"Since she started the company a few years ago. It's a matter of public record." Lark flipped her braid over her shoulder. "I'm not the only one."

"Stay here a sec," he ordered. The forensic team had packed up their gear. Crandall tramped toward them across the parking lot. After a brief conversation with the lead man, Crandall shook hands and returned to the car. "Okay, here's what's gonna happen. I'll call Esther's attorney in the morning. Meanwhile, I suggest you go home and take a look at your contracts. Figure out whether or not you have the authority to run her businesses, and call me."

"Me? Run the businesses?"

"Hey, the way I've got it figured, we're about through here. All that's left is the mop-up. With Esther dead, somebody's got to take over the operations. If Vic's right and she doesn't have any next of kin…Hey, even if he's wrong and she does…you're her partner. In my book, that makes you the person in charge."

"How can you be so callous, Bernie? Esther's been murdered."

Crandall studied the ground. "If I let it be personal, I couldn't do my job." He paused for a beat, then lifted his head. "There's just no telling how quick shutting down a business can affect the bottom line."

"Pretty darn fast," Lark admitted.

"That's what I figured, especially seeing as how we're at peak season. So unless you and all those other investors want to lose your shirts, I suggest you come up with a game plan and call me tomorrow."

Lark didn't know how to respond.

"Hey, Drummond, I'm tryin' to be nice here."

"Yeah, thanks."

Shadows shrouded the parking lot, and Elk Park's lights twinkled in the valley. In the background, one of Crandall's men uncoiled a hose from a spigot on the wall. Whistling a tune from Snow White and the Seven Dwarfs, he hosed the remnants of blood from the asphalt as casually as she might rinse bird droppings off a patio. Mop-up. Thank God Vic was gone.

Suddenly, Lark felt exhausted. "Am I free to go?"

"Sure," Crandall said, rolling his hand and gesturing grandly. "Be my guest." He waited until she'd walked around the patrol car, then called out, "Hey, don't forget to give me a call if you have any great revelations."

"I guarantee, you'll be the first to know."

As promised, Rachel was waiting to give her a ride up the hill. Lark found her parked around front, with the seat leaned back and jazz music drifting from the radio.

"Thanks for hanging around," Lark said, sliding onto the passenger seat.

"No problem." Rachel sat up and readjusted the seat. "How did it go?"

"Okay, I guess." Lark heard the tears in her voice before feeling the sting in her eyes. She tried fighting them back, but images of Esther crumpled in Vic's arms floated through her head. Images of pain, and blood, and death.

"Here." Rachel reached across and handed her a wad of tissues. "I saved you some."

Lark's tears flowed unchecked.

The drive to the Drummond was short, and Lark had barely composed herself before Rachel pulled the car up to the carriage house door and stopped. Stephen Velof hailed her from the hotel's porch. Lark cringed as he headed across the parking lot.

"I'll call you tomorrow, Rae," she said, climbing out of the Toyota. Shutting the door, she banged twice on the side. Rachel waved and pulled away.

"I was beginning to wonder if you ever planned to come back," Velof said. "What did you find out?"

"Nothing you want to know, Stephen." Lark started up the front steps. "Aren't you supposed to be off by now?"

"I was waiting for you. I was hoping we could resolve the coffee issue." He followed her toward the carriage house. "What don't I want to know?"

"I didn't have a chance to talk to Esther."

"What?" He reached out and steadied himself on the porch railing. "Why not? You gave me your word."

"Because Esther is dead, Stephen."

"Dead?" His face turned fish-belly white. "As in deceased?"

"As in 'as a doornail.'"

Velof hesitated for only a second. "Do they know who will be taking over her operation? Perhaps we could contact them?"

Pragmatic to the heart. Just like Crandall.

"Possibly me," she said, noting a faint ripple of disbelief

31

cross his face. "I'm supposed to call the attorney in the morning." She reached for the screen door. "Right now, I'm taking a bath."

"How will this affect the coffee delivery?" he persisted. "I did send someone to the grocery, as you suggested, but the coffee supply there is, well…rather limited, not to mention expensive and horrid tasting."

"I won't know anything until tomorrow, Stephen. Now, if that's all…?"

Velof glanced down. "There is one more thing."

Lark paused, her hand on the screen.

"Peter Jacobs hired a singer for the lounge."

Based on Stephen's critical tone, Lark guessed that he didn't approve of the new hire. But hiring lounge entertainment was Jacobs' responsibility, and he was good at it. "That's his job. What's the problem?"

"We can't afford to hire this girl."

"Why not? What's her fee?"

"It's not that, it's—"

"Just answer my question, Stephen," she snapped, tired of the melodrama. "What's her fee?"

Velof stiffened, balling his fists at his sides. "She wants fifty dollars a night and a place to live. Jacobs assigned her a vacant bed in the Manor House."

Elk Park, like the majority of resort areas, suffered from a shortage of low-cost housing. Seasonal workers could no longer afford to pay the high rents. Hotels and lodges could no longer afford to pay salaries high enough to compensate. The stalemate called for creative measures.

Lark solved the problem by providing her own on-site housing. Maids, wait staff, kitchen staff, and front desk help were assigned rooms in the Manor House. Beds were allocated on a first-come, first-served basis. Even Velof lived on site in a small apartment designated as the manager's quarters.

"I don't see the problem. Two hundred fifty dollars a week isn't out of line," Lark said. "And, if there's room in the Manor…"

"The woman doesn't have a green card."

Lark dropped her hand to her side, giving Velof her full attention. "Jacobs hired an illegal?"

Velof grinned a Cheshire smile. "A real songbird."

Lark's blood pressure rose a notch. "Is he insane?"

Colorado was notorious for harboring its share of illegal immigrants—mostly Mexican—by welcoming them into the minority segments of the communities spread up and down the Front Range. A business caught employing an illegal was subject to hefty fines and penalties, and, in some cases, the loss of a business license.

"We can't hire someone who doesn't hold a green card," Lark protested.

"That's what I said, but Jacobs considered it a special case."

"Special case, my tush. It's not worth the risk. I'll tell him myself. He'll just have to unhire the girl." Lark headed for the hotel.

"That's what I told him you'd say," Stephen crowed, scampering behind her. "But he insisted I speak with you before I fired her."

Something in Velof's tone stopped Lark in her tracks. What wasn't he telling her? "Does this singer have a name?"

Velof pivoted at the edge of the lawn. The glare from the streetlamp blotted out his features. He coughed.

"Her name, Stephen."

Velof scuffed the toe of his loafer along the asphalt curb. "Teresa. Teresa Cruz."

Chapter 4

Harboring had just taken on new meaning.

"Where is she now?" demanded Lark, anger bubbling inside her. Whether it was directed at Velof, Jacobs, Teresa, or at Esther for dying, Lark couldn't tell.

"She's in the lounge," Velof said, glancing at his watch. "Jacobs scheduled her on at eight."

Teresa needed to be fired. And she needed to be told about Esther. Not a job for Velof. The man showed about as much compassion as a hungry mountain lion. Talk about leading a lamb to slaughter.

Then there was Crandall, but he wanted to question Teresa in connection with Esther's murder. No compassion there, either.

Velof wet his lips. "I must point out, Lark, you're not exactly dressed to make a hotel appearance."

Lark glanced down at her clothes. By hotel policy—her policy—semiformal evening attire was required in the lobby areas after six o'clock. That meant coats and ties for men, and skirts or nice slacks for women. She was still wearing her shorts and flannel shirt, and both looked worse for wear.

"What time is it?"

"Ten till."

"Then I have time to change."

Velof nodded. "In the meantime, I'll inform Jacobs of your decision and apologize to our guests."

"That's okay. You've done your duty, Stephen," she said, smiling coldly. "I'll take it from here."

He stalked away, and she turned back toward the house.

Entering the bedroom, she peeled off her boots, heavy socks, flannel shirt, shorts, and T-shirt. After a quick swipe with a washcloth, she pulled on a pair of soft brown pants, a silk knit tank top, a cashmere sweater, and loafers. Then, yanking a brush through waist-length tangles, she braided her hair and secured the end with a soft black ponytail holder. By the time she crossed the parking lot to the Drummond, the temperature had dipped considerably.

There must be a front moving through, she thought, good on one hand, bad on the other. Colorado needed rain, but tomorrow afternoon kicked off the tenth annual Migration Alliance conference. Rain would have a definite negative impact on all of the scheduled bird-watching activities.

Lark reached the patio as strains of "Amor Prohibido" wafted through the French doors. She glanced at her watch. Why had they started early?

Teresa's clear, strong voice caressed the air, weaving a spell that wrapped itself around Lark. A number of others also seemed enthralled. The diners on the patio ceased talking, while patrons crowded the doors.

Lark shook off the spell and bounded up the steps to the main foyer. Peter Jacobs lounged against the doorjamb leading to the bar, watching Teresa's performance. A short, skinny man, he sported a trim beard and displayed great, if somewhat wrinkled, taste in clothing: pink oxford shirttails tucked hastily into a pair of belted chinos, pink-socked feet crammed into brown leather loafers.

"We need to talk," Lark said.

Peter started at her voice, his fingers moving nervously to his beard. "Lark!"

"My office. Now."

"Can't it wait until after the set?"

Lark poked her head inside the lounge. The tables and chairs were packed. "I guess it will have to."

She noticed Paul Owens sitting near the stage with his business partner, Katherine Saunders, and the tall blond woman from the Warbler. They were accompanied by an older gentleman with graying sideburns, who watched Teresa intently. When the girl launched into a reggae-enhanced rendition of "Bidi Bidi Bom Bom," a Latino chart topper, the gentleman danced in his seat.

Teresa gyrated onstage, bedecked in a high-waisted, short-skirted, bright pink sundress dotted with powder-blue flowers. The dress swirled as she shimmied, a look of rapture transforming her face. After three more songs, she ended the set with "God's Child," and the crowd demanded an encore. Teresa

35

promised to return in twenty minutes.

Once she'd escaped the stage, Lark snagged her and marched her and Jacobs back to the office. Velof was waiting for them. Lark waved everyone to chairs. Teresa and Peter sat together. Velof declined, and posted himself sentinel-like beside the door.

First things first. Lark scooted a chair next to Teresa's. "There's something I have to tell you."

Teresa's gaze darted from Jacobs to Velof, then cast about as though seeking an avenue of escape.

"Esther Mills is dead."

Teresa's head jerked back as if she'd been struck. Her dark eyes shone with pain, the type born from years of suffering. However, she showed no remorse, for the moment. "When? How?"

"Late this afternoon." Lark drew a deep breath, then exhaled. "She was murdered."

Teresa covered her face with her hands, but not before Lark spotted a glimmer of fear. What was she afraid of? Being in the United States alone, or that someone might accuse of her killing Esther?

Lark reached out and touched her shoulder. "I'm sorry."

Teresa jerked away. "I'm not."

Not quite the reaction she expected. Lark tried a different tack. "Police Chief Crandall wants to talk to you."

Teresa's body trembled. "I won't…I have nothing to say."

"I'm afraid you don't have a choice." Lark glanced at Jacobs. He kept his attention focused on Teresa, concern etched in deep lines around his eyes. Behind him, vigilant at the door, Velof looked bored.

Teresa's pink-tipped fingers picked at the edge of the wooden desk. "Mr. Velof must have told you."

"That you don't have a green card?"

"Yes."

"He did." Lark tried in vain to make eye contact with the girl. "Is that what you and Esther were arguing about? I overheard her threatening to send you home."

Teresa raised her chin defiantly. "Everyone heard her."

"Do you mind telling me what happened?"

The girl tossed her head like a headstrong filly. "My father arranged for my travel – we are a people at war. You must understand, he was frightened for me."

"Frightened of what?" Lark asked.

Teresa fired off a rapid volley of Spanish.

"I'm sorry. English, please. I don't speak your language that well." Lark looked at the others. "Unless someone else can translate?"

Jacobs shook his head, crossing his arms and turning sideways in his chair.

"She said her father didn't arrange the papers correctly," Velof said. "In fact, he screwed them up royally."

That it was Velof who spoke, Velof who understood her, surprised Lark. The Latin language seemed more suited to Jacobs than the straight-backed portrait she'd painted of the Drummond day manager.

"She says it was because he didn't want certain people alerted to the fact she was leaving the country," he continued.

"What do her papers say?" Lark asked.

Velof waited for Teresa's response, then cleared his throat. "She says they give her permission to be in the United States for six months. After that, she's forced to return to Mexico."

"Only, let me guess, she doesn't intend to go back."

"Eventually, I will," Teresa explained, "just not right away."

"Did Esther know that?"

"Yes." The girl spoke in Spanish again. This time, her words were barely audible.

"Esther promised Teresa's father that once Teresa was in the United States, they would arrange for her to obtain a green card," Velof said, pacing the narrow track of tile that separated the door from the chair, like a soldier on patrol paces the fence. "According to Teresa, Esther never followed through."

"That's right," Teresa said, continuing in Spanish.

"Apparently, Teresa's father paid Esther to help them, plus he supposedly gave Esther money that belonged to Teresa. Money she'd never received. She claims Esther lied to them from the beginning and used the money for the business, but that her father believes she's safe here."

"Safe from what?" An unsuitable romance? A childhood indiscretion?

It wasn't the idea of a father sending his daughter away that Lark found unfathomable. That sort of thing happened all the time, and for any number of reasons. When Lark turned fourteen, her father had shipped her off to boarding school, justifying his parental abdication by convincing himself—and anyone else who would listen—that it was for Lark's own good.

No, what Lark found unfathomable was the fear inherent in Mr. Cruz's decision to send Teresa away with Esther. He must have been seriously frightened to entrust his daughter to a stranger with no official credentials backing her up.

"I don't understand the danger."

"How much do you know about the revolution in Mexico?" Velof asked.

"I know there's been some civil unrest in the southern states, but—"

"Civil unrest?" Velof snorted. "More like civil war."

The vehemence in his voice unsettled Lark. "What do you know about it?"

"Enough." Velof stopped marching and sat down on the windowsill, arms stiff at his sides. "In 1994, a band of Indian farmers calling themselves the Zapatistas led an uprising against the Mexican government. They cited problems such as work, land distribution, housing, food, health care, education, etc. And they timed the rebellion to coincide with the ceremonies marking the first day of the North American Free Trade Agreement." He gripped the edge of the windowsill so hard his knuckles turned white. "One hundred forty-five Zapatistas and civilians died during that twelve-day siege. After that, the rebellion moved underground, and there's been only sporadic fighting between the guerrilla forces, the forces of the government, and the larger landholders. Still, war is war."

Jacobs, who hadn't said anything up to then, reached for Teresa's hand, "Teresa is a Tzotzil Mayan. Her father is an Indian coffee grower sympathetic to the Zapatista rebels. All the Indians want is the right to work and some land to grow their

38

crops on."

"My people are very poor," Teresa explained.

Velof snorted. "And whose fault is that? All your people need to do is tap into the resources. Yet every time the government tries to help, the Zapatistas contend the government's offer to control of the land. The government is not all bad."

"They are," Teresa insisted.

Lark turned to face Velof. "There must be some reason the people believe it is."

Velof cupped his hands, slapping them against his sleeves with a popping noise. "Just before NAFTA, the PRI repealed an article of the constitution that protected the communal land holdings of the Indian people."

"Who's the PRI?" Lark interrupted, curious how Velof knew so much about the political climate of southern Mexico.

"The Institutional Revolutionary Party," Teresa answered. "The ruling party."

"All the repeal did was open the door to privatization of the Indian communal property," Velof continued, "and most of the Indians already work their own plots of land."

Jacobs slid forward in his chair. "Don't you get it? It's the same thing that happened in the 1700s in the Scottish Highlands. The English government forced the Scots to privatize, pitting clan against clan. It destroyed their cultural base."

"No one in Chiapas is being forced to do anything," Velof said.

"No? What about La Mascara Roja?" Teresa shivered, and Jacobs draped a protective arm around her shoulders.

"Who?" Lark asked.

"La Mascara Roja," Velof scoffed. "The so-called 'red guard.' A group of opportunists, if you ask me."

Teresa straightened her carriage. "They are PRI gunmen."

"How are they any different than the masked rebels? Or the large landholders with their 'white guard,' for that matter? I wonder if you've ever considered that your people might benefit from a little civilizing."

"Stop," Lark ordered. "This is getting us nowhere."

Teresa mumbled something in Spanish.

Lark looked at Velof. "Care to translate?"

Velof shook his head.

Teresa flashed a haughty smile, then spoke directly to Lark. "In December of 1997, the PRI stole the coffee harvests of Las Abejas. Just before Christmas, they came back and killed forty-five women and children in Acteal. I was there. I got away, but my mother was killed."

Lark stared at Teresa. The girl had lost a parent and witnessed a massacre. Was that the reason her father had sent her to the United States, the reason he distrusted the Mexican government so much? "Does your father think you're in danger?"

Teresa bowed her head. "He made me leave because of what I saw."

Things were starting to make sense. It's natural to feel afraid with the Mexican army on your tail. "It's time we called your father, Teresa."

"No!" The girl squeezed Lark's hand tightly, making her wince. "The town's telephone…it is listened to by the government. It is not safe."

"Are you saying there's no way to reach your dad?"

"Sometimes he calls me." Teresa pulled her hand back and studied her nails.

Velof pushed away from the windowsill. "Let's get back to addressing the green card, shall we?"

Lark bristled. "Back off, Stephen." She stood and walked around the desk. While Jacobs nervously finger-combed his beard and Teresa fidgeted, Velof dusted his lapels. "How is it you know so much about what's happening in Chiapas, Stephen?"

Velof shrugged. "I worked a resort in Veracruz, a place called Fortin de las Flores."

"Yes, I know it," Teresa said.

Velof ignored her. "It's a beautiful little town, a former Spanish outpost."

"It has beautiful gardens there, and very sweet fruit," Teresa said.

Velof turned his back and faced the small window, looking

out over the Drummond lawns. "A lot of wealthy Mexican families own private homes there or visit the area on vacation. I worked at the Palacio, the largest resort club in town."

That explained how he understood Spanish.

"While I was there, guerrillas attacked a small military post near the city. They had heard that the president of Mexico was staying at the Palacio, and they stormed the club. I was held hostage. One of my friends died."

"Lo siento," Teresa whispered.

Velof glared at the girl. "The Zapatistas, the PRD as they're called, claim they're fighting for freedom, for a better government, for more democracy. I think they just want more for themselves."

"That's not true." Teresa leaned toward him, hatred marring her face. "They fight for the people, for the women and children."

Lark recognized a Mexican standoff when she saw one. Velof and his biases versus Teresa and hers. Lark found herself poised in the middle with no idea which side to take.

A knock at the door shattered the strained silence. Lark breathed a sigh of relief at the interruption. "Yes? Come in."

The bartender stuck his head in the door and flashed a fistful of fingers. "Teresa's on in five."

"Her encore has been canceled," Velof told him.

Lark blasted him with a frosty stare, then spoke to the stunned barkeep. "Tell the crowd she's not feeling well. I'll explain it to you later."

"What's there to explain?" Velof said. "She can't perform. We'd be in direct violation of—"

Lark slammed her hand against the desk, causing the others to jump and the bartender to slam the door. "Need I remind you that I run the Drummond, and you work for me?"

Jacobs and Teresa shook their heads. Velof's ears turned pink.

To break the tension, Lark tried tapping Crandall's dirge on the desktop. It came out "Here Comes the Bride." Lark stilled her fingers. "Look, all of you, I've had a long day. And, as much as I hate to admit it, Teresa, Stephen's right. I know about the

41

green card. I can't let you work."

"But I have no money."

"I understand that, but…" Lark smiled sympathetically. "You have to look at this from my point of view. Technically, I should be calling immigration."

"No!" Teresa's eyes took on a sheen. "Please, you can't!"

Lark raised both hands to calm the girl. "I won't. I promise." She shot a glance at Velof. "And neither will anyone else in this room. But you've got to help me. You've got to give me some time to straighten things out."

First there was the issue of immigration; then there was the issue of Crandall to settle. She would have to call him eventually.

"She can stay in the Manor House," Jacobs said. "I've already assigned her a room."

Teresa pouted. "But what about money?"

"You have fifty dollars coming from tonight. That should cover you for a day or two."

"But I want to work."

"Well, you can't. Not right now." Lark sat back in her chair. "Peter, show Teresa to her room and pay her the money we owe her in cash. Meanwhile, I'll do some checking tomorrow on the status of your immigration visa."

Teresa rose without another word and swiveled her hips to the door. Jacobs followed her out. Lark glanced at Velof. "She can be quite the prima donna."

"Hmpf," he replied.

Lark sighed. Somehow she had to mend the fence. She needed his help right now. "Look, I'm sorry if I offended you. You know how much I rely on your judgment."

When he still didn't respond, she headed for the door. There was only so much sucking up she could do.

"Frankly, she's what I'd call a chipe."

Lark frowned and turned back. "As in Chipe Coffee? Isn't that Spanish for warbler?"

"Yes, but I'm choosing to apply the slang definition."

"Which is?"

"A major-league spoiled brat."

DEATH OF A SONGBIRD

Chapter 5

After a soak in the tub, Lark gratefully climbed into bed, waking the next morning to sunshine warming her face. The sunlight dappled the quilt in dalmatian spots, and she stretched, basking in the warm rays before remembering that Esther Mills was dead.

The realization hit her full force. Her friend and partner was gone—murdered—in a senseless act of violence. And for what? A few measly dollars?

Death always surprised Lark. Even when she saw it coming, it broadsided her with its callous disregard; how it took only a moment to forever change the lives of those left behind to mourn.

When William Tanager had died, she had stood vigil with Miriam. Then, at the last possible moment, in fear of her own mortality, Lark had bolted, leaving Miriam in the clutches of her wicked stepdaughters.

This summer, when she'd stumbled upon the reporter's body in The Thicket, Lark had screamed. Bottom line, she didn't handle death well.

Thank heavens she'd found the strength to keep it together yesterday. Somehow she'd managed to keep her lunch down and stick by Rachel, who has charged in where only braver women dared go.

Lark rolled over and gazed out the bedroom window. By now, everyone in Elk Park knew about the murder. Bad news traveled fast in a small town. And by now, the old guard would have started the telephone tree and stocked Vic Garcia's refrigerator with enough frozen casseroles to feed Denver's transient population for a week. Since Esther had no known heirs, it would fall to Vic to plan the memorial service.

On the other hand, the Chipe Coffee Company, the Warbler Café, and Teresa were her problems. Lark glanced at the bedside clock. It was still too early to call the attorney Crandall had told her to contact.

Stumbling out of bed, Lark stripped off her pajamas and

made the requisite pit stop. Then, donning a pair of soft blue jeans, a white T-shirt, and tennis shoes, she headed to the kitchen. In the hoopla, she'd forgotten to shore up her personal coffee supply. A quick tour of the cupboards proved them bare of any other caffeine-laced substance.

Well, there's coffee at the Drummond. She stared out the kitchen window. And there's Velof at the Drummond. Nix that idea.

Lark weighed the other options. With the Warbler closed, she was left with the diner, the grocery store, or Bird Haven. Lark opted for Bird Haven.

Grabbing a jacket—more out of habit than necessity—she made a dash for the truck. The name of the game was Avoiding Velof. Sure enough, as she pulled the truck into the driveway, he tried flagging her down from the patio. Unwilling to scrub toilets, she pretended not to see him, peeling out of the parking lot in a spurt of sand. Whatever he wanted would keep.

The drive to Bird Haven took five minutes. A quick burst up Devil's Gulch, then a left under the overhead sign on to Raptor House Road. The private drive, fenced on both sides, meandered through a meadow sprinkled with tansy, aster, and fireweed. A cluster of buildings squatted in the distance.

The entire ranch encompassed twenty-five hundred acres of prime real estate situated at the base of Lumpy Ridge, a popular rock-climbing and recreational area that belonged to Rocky Mountain National Park. Climbing was restricted on the buttresses during the peregrine breeding season, but today the cliff area swarmed with climbers. Lark's ankle throbbed at the sight.

The ranch house perched on top of a small knoll. Large and sprawling, it had been built in the late 1800s by an enterprising cattle rancher, who later sold it to Miriam and Will. Behind the house sprawled the Raptor House, a seven-building rehabilitation center for injured birds. The structures and the land were part of Bird Haven, but the Park Service handled the daily operations.

Lark parked the truck beside the green Toyota, jumped out, and wandered around the house to the back door. "Hello?" she called. "Anybody home?"

Rachel hailed her from the kitchen. "Come in, come in. How are you today?"

"I could use a cup of coffee."

"I just made some, fresh-brewed."

Lark filled an oversized mug and splashed in a dollop of cream. Cupping the mug in her hands, she savored the smell, allowing the steam to penetrate her sinuses before taking a sip.

Rachel popped four slices of bread into the toaster, grabbed the jam and butter, and offered Lark a small plate and butter knife. "Here."

Lark helped herself to toast, then settled in at the breakfast nook table. "You'll never guess what happened last night."

"Nothing bad, I hope."

"It depends on how you look at it." Slathering the toast with strawberry jam, she told Rachel about the scene with Teresa. "Velof was downright Gestapo-like."

Rachel looked thunderstruck. "Teresa's an illegal immigrant?" She shook her head. "Lark, you're taking a huge risk letting her stay at the Manor."

Setting her knife on the edge of her plate, Lark reached for a napkin. "What else could I do? I couldn't just throw her out. She's practically a kid."

"Have you called the attorney like Crandall told you to?"

"He's not in until nine."

A ruckus from the dining room drew their attention. The adjoining door banged open, and a streak of white swooped toward them. Perky, Miriam's cinnamon teal parakeet, made a beeline for Rachel's hair.

Rachel covered her head. "Get away!"

The bird landed on the curtain rod above the table, tipped his head, and said, "Perky wants a hair."

"Who let you in?" Rachel shrieked and draped a napkin over her head, knotting it under her chin like a scarf.

The bird dived. Rachel swatted the air. Perky buzzed around for another pass. Stooping like a miniature bird of prey, he dove at Rachel's head and came up triumphant with a long strand of auburn hair.

"Ouch," Rachel said, yanking off the napkin and rubbing her head. "Are you satisfied now?"

Lark burst out laughing.

Rachel glared at her. "I hate that bird."

"Oh my," Cecilia Meyer said, bustling into the room. She shooed Perky to a perch above the kitchen stove. "I'm afraid it was all my fault that he got in. Will you ever forgive me, Rachel? I'm just so flustered. I wasn't paying attention."

Her sister, Dorothy MacBean, who had followed her in, bobbed her head in joint apology. The two women looked nearly identical: midsixties, permed hair, gray eyes, pale skin. Today they wore matching pedal pushers and two-toned shirts in opposite patterns of pink and blue.

"Gertie's coming behind us," Dorothy added. "We've been looking for you, Lark."

Lark tapped her fingers against the side of her coffee mug. "I take it you heard about Esther."

"Then, you do know. I told you so, Cecilia."

"Know?" Rachel blurted, obviously prepared to fill them in on yesterday's happenings. Lark flapped her arms, signaling her not to say anything more. Rachel ignored her. "We were there."

"Oh my," Cecilia said, her eyes growing rounder. "You mean you witnessed the murder?"

Rachel shook her head. "Not me, but Lark did."

Lark groaned.

"Really?" Dorothy asked, crossing to the table. "You saw the killer?"

"Yes and no. I saw him through the scope." Lark drew her knees up and propped them against the edge of the breakfast bar.

"Well, are you going to tell us the story or not?" Gertie asked, storming into the room, black hair bobbing around her face. She'd managed to squeeze herself into a tight, knit short set that made her look like a human corn dog.

Rachel choked on her coffee.

Lark pursed her lips and toyed with the edge of her napkin.

"Well? Spill the beans."

"There isn't much to spill," Lark told them.

"At least cough up what you know."

The women clustered around the table, like chickens waiting for crumbs. There was no escape. Lark searched for where to start. "I was teaching Rae how to use a spotting scope, when we saw this unusual-looking bird…some kind of warbler, I think…and—"

"What were its markings?" Cecilia interrupted.

"Oh please," Gertie said, dragging up a kitchen stool. "You can ask her that later. Let's try and stay focused here."

Lark sipped her coffee. "Actually, I've never seen a warbler like this one before. It—"

"Forget the bird," Gertie said. "What about the murder?"

Cecilia slipped onto the bench seat beside Lark and patted her arm. "You can come back to the warbler later, dear."

Lark smiled. "So, where was I?"

"You saw the bird," Cecilia prompted.

Dorothy swatted her sister's arm.

"Well, she did."

"And it flew," Lark said, "so I tried tracking it with the scope. Unfortunately, the height was set for Rachel, and I swung the dam thing too far to the left. That's when I saw the killer stab Esther."

"Oh my!"

"Were you able to identify him?" Gertie asked.

Lark rubbed the edge of the table. "I didn't get that good a look. He was wearing a mask, with some lettering on it—"

Gertie leaned forward. "What kind of lettering?"

"You're beginning to sound like Crandall." Lark closed her eyes and tried visualizing the scene. "There was an E and a Z… that's all I'm sure of."

Dorothy raised her hand for permission to speak. "Do you remember how many letters there were?"

"Four. I'm sure there were four."

"Absolutely positive?" Cecilia asked.

Lark made a face. "I'm fairly certain. There may have been five, but—"

"No," Rachel said. "You were right the first time. There were four."

"How would you know?" Gertie asked. "Lark was the one looking through the scope."

"Because, I wrote the letters down."

Lark's stomach flip-flopped. She uncurled her legs and sat up. "You did?"

"Yes, don't you remember? You told me to take notes while you called out the markings on the bird we spotted. I thought it was sort of odd when you blurted out those letters, but I jotted them down in your field book anyway."

Lark grabbed Rachel's arm. "Where's the book now?"

"Upstairs," Rachel said, disengaging her arm and scooting out from behind the breakfast nook table. "I carried it up from the peninsula. I must have shoved it in my pocket when I checked Esther's pulse, because I found it after I got home. I'll get it."

While she went to retrieve the notebook, Dorothy claimed possession of her seat. "So what happened next?"

"Dorothy," Cecilia said. "Don't be such a vulture."

"Well, it's not fair to stop in the middle of a story."

"Nothing happened," Lark said. "I yelled for Rachel to call nine-one-one, then we ran up from the lake and found Vic holding Esther in the parking lot." Lark hugged herself, rocking back and forth in her seat. "Rachel checked to see if Esther was breathing, but she was already dead. Then Crandall arrived."

"Oh, you poor thing," Dorothy said.

Cecilia draped an arm across Lark's shoulders and patted her arm.

Rachel rejoined them, cracking open the notebook. "E, Z, L, N. Does that mean anything to anyone?"

They all looked at each other, then shook their heads.

"Elk something or other," Dorothy suggested.

"What could the Z stand for?" Rachel reached for a sheet of scratch paper. "Zoo, Zebra—"

Cecilia perked up. "How about Zen?"

"Oh, please," Gertie huffed. "We could spend all day trying to decode those letters."

She had a point, thought Lark. Decoding the Z limited their choices, but, if the letters were initials, they could still stand for anything.

"Poor Esther," Dorothy murmured.

Gertie snorted. "She's not the only poor person in this room."

A shocked silence followed. Everyone stared at Gertie.

"I'm only stating the truth." Gertie tugged at the cuffs on her shorts. "I just don't know what we're going to do."

A shrill note had crept into Gertie's voice, and she ended on a wail that jolted Lark up out of her seat. Gertie was worried about money.

Lark tapped her watch face. "I don't know about we, but I'm going to call the attorney, then Crandall. He'll want to know about the letters, and he told me the Warbler could be reopened in the next couple of days. Whose job that will be depends on what the partnership agreements say."

The women followed her into the family room en masse, crowding around while she looked up the attorney's phone number. Lark backed them off a respectable distance before placing the actual call, then armed herself with Miriam's ski pole, which doubled as a walking stick and had been leaning against the wall next to the phone table, to keep them at bay.

The attorney's secretary answered on the second ring. "Mr. Arquette's office."

Gil Arquette specialized in corporate law. After practicing for twenty years in a downtown Denver firm, he'd semiretired to the peaceful surroundings of Elk Park. Nowadays, local businesses represented the lion's share of his clientele. Esther Mills is—had been—his premier client.

"Good morning, Ms. Drummond. What can I do for you?"

"Call me Lark, Mr. Arquette – and I need some help."

"I heard. Bernie Crandall called me this morning."

Lark gestured to the others, indicating he knew about the murder.

"Horrible thing. Just horrible," he continued. "What I can't figure out is, who would have wanted her dead?"

"Probably someone after the bank receipts," Lark ventured.

"Except that she wasn't robbed."

"Excuse me?"

Rachel, Dorothy, Cecilia, and Gertie leaned forward at the

note of surprise. Lark waved them off with the ski pole.

"How do you know that, Mr. Arquette?" He hadn't given her permission to call him Gil.

"Well, according to Bernie, they found the bank deposit lying on the ground a few feet away from her body. He thinks someone wanted her dead."

"What's going on?" Gertie whispered. "What's he saying?"

Lark cupped her hand over the mouthpiece. "He says it wasn't a robbery. That someone intentionally killed Esther without taking her bank deposit."

A buzz rose from the women. Lark plugged her free ear and hunched over the receiver. "Do the police have any suspects?"

"The usual. Business associates, family, and heirs. You are aware she left a will."

Lark's chest tightened. "No, I didn't know that."

"According to the partnership agreements, you and Esther are, or should I say, were equal partners. There is no survivorship clause in the contracts. You still own approximately forty percent of the Chipe Coffee Company, which encompasses the Warbler Café. The other investors, Dorothy MacBean, Cecilia Meyer, and Gertie Tanager, own a combined twenty percent share. Esther's heir receives the other forty percent."

"What are you saying, Mr. Arquette?"

"I'm saying that, for the moment, you and the others are free to reopen the business."

"That's great news." Lark flashed an okay sign to the others.

"But, hold on there, missy. It's imperative you hear me out. I said 'for the moment.' Right now it requires that three of you swing a majority—you and two of the others. However, once the will is probated, it may be a totally different story."

Lark flailed the ski pole in the air, trying to shush the others. "What do you mean, Mr. Arquette?"

"Esther's heir can choose to petition the courts for company control."

"How will that affect us?"

"If he loses? Not at all. If he wins? You'll be knocked back to silent partner status."

Lark banged the ski pole on the floor. The others stopped talking.

"It's a remote possibility," said Arquette, rustling more papers, "but all of you did grant Esther stewardship of the businesses, thereby opening the front door for her heir to petition. Whether or not he does remains to be seen, as does whether or not he could triumph in such an action."

As far as Lark knew, there was only one likely candidate for heir. "Are you telling me this because you've already talked to Vic and he told you he planned to sue?"

Arquette cleared his throat. "I know as well as you that Vic and Esther were living together, but, in spite of that fact, she didn't leave him a dime."

"Then who's the heir?"

"Paul Owens, at the Migration Alliance."

Chapter 6

"Paul Owens?" Lark could have understood Esther's leaving her worldly possessions to the Alliance. She loved birds, especially migratory birds. But why Owens instead of the organization? "Did he know?"

Arquette chuckled. "Bernie Crandall asked me the same question. To be honest, I don't know if he knew anything before I called him this morning. Do I think your new partner killed Esther for her money? Not a chance."

There was a long silence, punctuated by the shak shak shak of a Steller's jay and the hum of the kitchen refrigerator. Rachel, Gertie, Dorothy, and Cecilia seemed to be holding their breath.

"I guess that about wraps things up," Lark said finally.

"Feel free to call back if you need anything."

"Wait, there is one more thing, Mr. Arquette. What do you know about immigration law?" Lark explained the situation with Teresa. "Is there anything that can be done, any way we can help her?"

Arquette made a clicking noise. "For the record, I'm not an expert in the field."

"Acknowledged."

"She might be able to apply to INS for an 'unskilled worker' permit, but the waiting list for obtaining one runs into the years. There's a slim chance she could qualify as a 'skilled worker,' provided you have a job tailor-made to her qualifications. Does she have any special job skills?"

"She's a superior waitress, and she can sing."

"Unfortunately, neither one qualifies."

Lark racked her brain. Was she overlooking something? Teresa had worked on her father's coffee farm for years. Maybe she knew something about import or exportation. "What constitutes special?"

"Let's just say, sports stars don't have a problem obtaining permits. Neither do engineers, computer specialists, scientists...you get the drift. And understand, of course, that either option hinges on the current state of her visa."

"How so?"

"If her visa's current, we can make application and ask for an extension of her visitor papers. It would mean she couldn't work, but she could remain in the U.S., at least until an immigration permit is granted or until she reapplies for an extension."

"What if her visa's already expired?" A distinct possibility. This was August. Esther's last buying trip to Chiapas had been in December.

"According to the new laws, she'd be forced to return to Mexico and live outside the U.S. for several years. After that, she can reapply."

It was a moot point. Teresa would never agree to go back to Chiapas. She'd disappear first.

"What happens if we do nothing?"

"She may never get caught. And, even if you employ her, you may never get fined."

Lark felt a surge of hope. "Why's that?"

"INS has their hands full. The state of Colorado hosts approximately forty-five thousand illegal immigrants versus seventeen assigned INS agents. Immigration's fighting an uphill battle."

"Thanks for the help, Mr. Arquette." Lark signed off and immediately dialed Bernie Crandall. He answered his own phone on the third ring. "Yo?"

"Bernie, it's Lark. I just finished talking with Arquette. He told me that once you gave the go-ahead, we could reopen the Warbler."

"Consider it done, Drummond. The boys didn't need long inside."

"Great." Images of powder-covered counters flashed through her head. "I'll need Esther's set of keys."

"Sure thing. You can pick 'em up at the station."

"When?"

"How 'bout tomorrow? Say around nine? If I'm not here, I'll leave them with the sergeant at the front desk."

"Great," she said again. "And, hey, I know what the letters on the ski cap were." She explained how Rachel had written them down in the field book. "E, Z, L, N. None of us have a clue what they stand for."

"Thanks, Drummond, that's a big help. Who's us?"

Lark hesitated. "Gertie, Dorothy, Cecilia, Rachel, and me."

"Geez, so how long before all of Elk Park knows?"

Lark glanced at the others. "We'll keep it to ourselves."

"You might, but there's no way Dorothy's keeping her trap shut."

He had a point. "Look, bear with me, I have something else for you, too."

"Shoot." He sounded bored.

"I know where Teresa is." She filled him in on coming home and finding Teresa singing in the lounge. "It was late by the time we were done talking, so I sent her to bed in the Manor House."

"What's the room number?"

"Twelve."

"You should have called me last night."

"I didn't think—"

"Guess not. Is that everything, Drummond, or can you name the killer, too?"

"Sarcasm doesn't become you, Bernie." This was not shaping up to be the best time to ask him about the case, but it was now or never. "I just have a question. Arquette said you'd eliminated robbery as a motive in Esther's murder. Is that true?"

"He told you that, did he?"

"Yeah. Is it true?"

Crandall tapped a rhythm on his desk that carried across the phone line. "What's it to you, Drummond?"

"I'm curious, okay?" It was the truth. "Maybe I want to know because I witnessed her murder. She was my friend, my business partner. I just want some information."

"You're sure you're not just paranoid?"

Lark stiffened. "On a fishing expedition, Bernie?"

"Touché."

"En garde."

Crandall laughed. "Let's call a truce. You know I can't tell you anything."

She knew, but it didn't stop her from wondering if their

suspect lists matched. After her conversation with Arquette, Paul Owens topped her list. Teresa came next, with Vic a distant possibility. She wondered if her own name appeared anywhere on Crandall's list. "Why not give me the media version?"

"I'm not talkin' to them either." He paused. "Look, before I forget, Vic called. He wants to hold a memorial service for Esther at the café on Saturday afternoon. You got any problems with that?"

Lark placed her hand over the mouthpiece and conferred with the others.

"I think it's all right," Dorothy said.

Gertie came back with a question. "How much revenue would be lost?"

Always the bottom line, Lark thought.

"I can see I'm going to have to discuss this with my partners. Can I get back to you, Bernie?"

"Not a problem. Just let me know."

Lark hung up the phone. "Forget the money, Gertie. This is about doing the right thing." She turned to Cecilia. "How do you feel about it?"

"It's fine with me, as long as he doesn't plan on scattering her ashes there."

Gertie made a face. "Get real."

"I'm dead serious. When Bob, my father-in-law, died, God rest his soul, Mrs. Meyer, that's my mother-in-law, wanted his ashes scattered along the shores of Whitmore Lake. Well, you can imagine how the local homeowners reacted, not to mention his Methodist relatives. But Mrs. Meyer was dead set on the idea, and argued her way to city hall. Thank heavens, she eventually lost."

"So, did they force interment?" Lark asked.

Cecilia's face pinked up, and she shuddered. "It was truly the most embarrassing thing. You see, after her request was denied, Mrs. Meyer held a funeral, complete with urn and urn bearers and flowers. Everyone thought she'd buried Bob at the Whitmore Lake cemetery. Then, several years later, Dorothy and I paid her a visit. You remember, don't you, Dorothy?"

"How could I forget?"

"Mrs. Meyers showed us in, and for once seemed happy to see me. You see, I don't think she ever really approved of my marriage to her Jimmy."

"What happened next?" Rachel asked.

"She served tea in the living room. It was a massive space, with a fireplace and two large windows that looked out over the lake. I remember her standing in a pool of light, gesturing with flourish toward the windows, and announcing, 'And there's Bob.'"

"She's scattered him anyway?" Lark asked.

"Oh no, dear."

"That's what she'd always intended to do," Dorothy said.

"But she hadn't." Cecilia waved a finger at Dorothy. "Instead, she'd kept him, propping his ashes beside the mantel in a taped-up white cardboard box."

"And she'd printed Bob in bright blue calligraphy across the front," added Dorothy.

Gertie paled. "You're kidding, right?"

"I wouldn't joke about something like that. My father-in-law was a wonderful man."

"And your mother-in-law was a fruitcake."

"Dorothy!"

"Face it, Cecilia. She was nuttier than a peanut roll."

"Whatever happened to Bob?" Lark asked, morbid curiosity getting the better of her.

"When Mrs. Meyer died, we buried them together. Bob would have wanted it that way."

"Well, Esther deserves a proper send off" Lark said. "And with a stipulation that Vic doesn't scatter her ashes among the bird feeders, the Warbler would be the appropriate place."

They all agreed.

"What comes next?" Cecilia asked.

Four pairs of eyes turned to Lark.

"We make a to-do list."

Listing was a legacy from her mother. Elizabeth Drummond made lists of groceries to buy, phone calls to make, appointments to keep, and errands to run. She made lists for the gardener, the chef, and Lark's nanny. She made lists because—

as a mother, the wife of Senator Nathan Drummond, and the president of the East Haddam, Connecticut, Junior League—Elizabeth relished organization.

Lark had refined the technique. She listed rarely, mostly birds. But, when she did, rather than making multiple lists, she used a column system, grouping items of importance in outline form on a single page.

At the top of a sheet of paper, she scribbled "Warbler Café," then jotted down the number one and wrote "personnel" beside it. Not counting Teresa, the Warbler Café had three part-time employees—Matt, Scott, and Lisa—all college students home on summer break. According to the posted schedule, Matt and Lisa worked Fridays and weekends. Scott worked weekdays, except Mondays, when the Warbler was closed. Teresa worked every shift, or had until today. Lark wrote their names in the "personnel" column, then drew a line through Teresa's name.

"We need someone to oversee general operations: bookkeeping, payroll, ordering, that sort of thing. And someone will need to cover daily ops: roasting, grinding, brewing coffee, etc. Anyone willing to volunteer?"

Rachel pushed herself up from the couch. "You can count me out of this discussion, so I'll go make some sandwiches."

"Scratch Rae." Lark hadn't figured she'd volunteer. Rachel was leaving in a couple of weeks, going back to her job as a top designer for the New York City-based marketing firm, Images Plus. Besides, even if she stayed, she telecommuted to work on a daily basis, sometimes seven days a week. She wasn't a partner. And she didn't have time to help out much, anyway. "Anyone else?"

Gertie raised both hands in the universal sign for surrender. A dental hygienist for Elk Park's lone DDS, her weekdays were spent cleaning coffee stains off other people's teeth. "I can't do it, either."

"But you could help on weekends," Lark said, jotting Gertie's name down and writing "Sat/Sun" beside it.

Lark scribbled her own name next. Better to volunteer for a job than get stuck with one she would hate. She was tied up at the Drummond Hotel on most days, but her hours were flexible, and she did have business experience. "I don't mind overseeing the general ops."

"Which leaves us with the day-to-day operation?" Dorothy crooked a finger at her sister, and the women huddled together in whispered conversation. Lark prayed they were equal to the task.

"We'll do it," announced Cecilia. "But this week poses a problem. The Migration Alliance convention kicks off this evening."

Which meant all four of them had additional obligations.

Dorothy served as MA's local program director. Cecilia pinch-hit backup. The Drummond, designated MA headquarters, was hosting tonight's kickoff party, Friday night's banquet, and next Thursday's wrap-up barbeque. In addition, Lark was slated to lead several birding field trips during the week, and there was an all-day volunteers hike on Sunday which was mandatory for everyone.

"Why don't we just wait until next weekend to reopen the store?" suggested Dorothy. "It will give us more time to prepare, and—"

"No," interrupted Gertie. "Think of the revenues. Think of how much money we'd lose."

"How much?" Dorothy looked to Lark for the answer.

Lark fingered her braid. "The only way to really know is to look at the books. Barring that…" She shrugged. "Do you want my educated guess?"

Dorothy nodded.

"It's the busy season, so… I'd say the store could gross several thousand."

"See?" Gertie said. "I was right. We can't afford to stay closed, or, for that matter, to host Esther's memorial."

Everyone ignored Gertie's last comment.

"Can we hire someone to supervise?" Cecilia asked, as Rachel carried a large tray in from the kitchen. Everyone looked at her.

"What?"

"Nothing," Cecilia said.

"How do you feel about helping out family?" Gertie asked.

Rachel glanced at Lark. "Is this a trick question?"

Lark nodded. "We need someone to supervise at the Warbler on Sunday."

"It's only one day," Dorothy said.

Rachel bobbled the tray. "No. Absolutely not."

"Oh, please reconsider," Cecilia implored. "We're desperate."

Lark leaned back in her chair and watched Rachel cave.

"I know I'm going to regret this," she mumbled. More loudly she said, "Okay, since there's no other way, I'll cover Sunday. How—"

Cecilia clapped her hands.

"However—"

Gertie sneered. "I knew there'd be a catch."

Rachel banged the tray down on the coffee table, bouncing half-sandwiches off their plates. "As I was saying, someone else will have to come in and close out the register. I don't want to be responsible for the money."

"Done," Lark said.

"And you'll need to find someone else to cover any scheduling conflicts or crises."

"Understood." Lark added a note to her list. "Consider yourself a token supervisor."

Rachel rolled her eyes. "What's everyone want to drink?"

Dorothy glanced at her watch. "Is it that late already? Oh goodness, conference registration opens in an hour. We have to go."

Cecilia sprang to her feet and smoothed the front of her pedal pushers. "I must say, I do feel better now that we have a plan."

Four hours later, Lark surveyed the Drummond patio with satisfaction. The cash bars were in place, the hors d'oeuvre table set, and chairs scattered strategically about. Even Velof appeared calm. Earlier, he'd been a mess.

Lark had returned from Bird Haven, changed into a pair of khaki pants, and devoted the afternoon to putting out fires. The coffee supply was dangerously low, so she'd ordered an overnight delivery of Song Bird Coffee from the American

Birding Association in Colorado Springs. Expensive, but organic.

Two maids were still out with the flu, and three of the kitchen staff had called in sick. Velof triggered a mild panic with talk about an outbreak of Legionnaires' disease, and Lark had spent over an hour convincing staff members it was safe to stay and work.

The most recent problem cropped up at three, when four departing guests didn't check out, leaving four incoming guests without rooms for the night. She was still working on that one.

"Everything looks perfect," Dorothy said, coming up behind her. "Did you remember to order lights for the podium?"

"Yes, Dee. Maintenance set them up an hour ago. Stop worrying."

Dorothy had changed from her pedal pushers into a sleek black pants suit. From underneath the sleeveless jacket peeked a short-sleeved pink shirt with a wide ruffled collar. A name tag in a plastic holder dangled against her chest at a rakish angle.

"You look terrific." Lark gave her two thumbs-up. "Everything's going to go fine."

"We can only pray." Dorothy glanced skyward.

Lark eyed the clouds. Earlier in the day, the sky had threatened rain. Dark thunderheads had rolled over the mountain peaks, bringing jagged flashes of lightning that speared toward the earth. Not a drop had fallen, and the storm had moved past. Now, only a wake of puffy white clouds remained to gather the sunset.

"Even the heavens fear Paul Owens," Dorothy said.

Lark cocked her head. "What do you mean by that?"

"He's very demanding."

That informational tidbit didn't bode well for the Chipe Coffee Company partnership. Lark had only met him once, at a promotional fund-raiser in McAllen, Texas. He'd seemed nice enough then. "What else do you know about him?"

"For one thing, he writes his speeches days in advance and practices them incessantly. I must have heard tonight's comments and set of introductions six times—once or twice yesterday, and at least four times today already." Dorothy glanced around to see if anyone was listening, then leaned in closer to Lark. "And, I can tell you something else, Lark. Paul Owens is only a figurehead. It's Katherine who holds the reins, and that woman makes the devil quake."

"She can't be that bad."

"With God as my witness," Dorothy said, raising her right hand and pretending to place her left on a Bible. "She's a witch with a capital B."

Lark added the information to what she already knew. Katherine, the only daughter of a prominent birder, shared her father's passion for all things avian. It was he who had provided the seed money to found the Migration Alliance, and she who had placed Paul in the organizational driver's seat.

"Don't look now," Dorothy said. "But here comes Stephen. What do you suppose the problem is?"

Velof's loafers clicked a staccato on the flagstones, hailing his arrival. Lark spun around. "What's up, Stephen?"

Dashing in a black Armani knockoff, he ruined the effect by sputtering, "People are starting to show up in the lobby, and, if I may say so, some of them are quite inappropriately dressed."

Lark could imagine. Most of the people she had seen were dressed in bright green MA T-shirts emblazoned with a white ptarmigan. "How so?"

"We have men in shorts, women in tank—" Velof stopped short, his eyes scanning Lark's attire.

She tugged at the straps of her silk knit top and brushed nonexistent dirt from the seat of her khaki pants. "These are birders, Stephen. They've come here to walk the mountain trails and look at the fauna. I think we can relax the rules for a couple of days."

"What about our other guests? The ones who aren't interested in birds, but in the more civilized customs of humanity?"

"They can dress up and eat in the dining room."

"You're setting a dangerous precedent."

"Sometimes you have to bend the rules."

Chapter 7

At five o'clock sharp, with the sun drooping in the summer sky, Dorothy MacBean opened the doors and five hundred people flooded the patio. A small quartet played valiantly in one corner, fighting to be heard above the chatter. From experience, Lark knew that many of the attendees only saw each other once a year at the MA convention or another birding event, and stories of spotting a bird, field trips, and hitting a landmark number abounded. In search of downtime, she clustered near the bar with a group of Elk Park Ornithological Chapter members.

Harry Eckles, one of her better friends and a longtime EPOCH member, lounged against the stone railing, stretching out his long legs. "I, for one, don't want to hear any more about Esther. I want to hear about the bird you saw."

"Ja, me, too," Eric Linenger said, joining them with a cold beer in hand. Having shed his park ranger uniform for chinos and a short-sleeved shirt, the tall Norwegian looked like he'd stepped out fo an Abercrombie & Fitch advertisement. A light breeze ruffled his brown hair, molding a thin cotton shirt against his well-formed pecs. Blue eyes gazed at her down a long, thin nose.

His gaze traveled her length. Lark's heart pounded beneath her silk blouse. Self-consciously, she raised her hand to her throat. It had been a while since a man had looked at her that way.

An elbow jab to the ribs nearly doubled her over and jolted her back to reality. What had she been thinking? Eric Linenger was the most eligible, most sought-after bachelor in Elk Park. Why would he be interested in her?

"Go ahead, dear," Cecilia said, tucking her arm back to her side. "Tell us."

"Well," Lark coughed and patted her chest. "I've never seen a bird like it. It was some kind of warbler, small, with a red throat, a red face, and a black cap." She expounded on the details, recalling the markings as best she could without her field notebook. She'd left it at Bird Haven. She made a mental note to retrieve it later. Bernie Crandall needed to see it.

"You've just described a red-faced warbler," Harry said.

"That's impossible," Andrew Henderson scoffed, popping a miniature egg roll into his mouth and tugging at the belt around his extra-wide girth. "There's never been a sighting in Colorado."

"You're wrong," Harry said. "Schottler and Stachowiak spotted one in Wheat Ridge in 1993. Schottler even got a picture."

Lark felt vindicated. Leave it to a biology professor to collect that kind of data.

"Okay, one sighting," Henderson conceded. "One." He held up a pudgy finger. "Elk Park's just too far out of the red-faced warbler's northern range to make it feasible."

"What is the range?" Cecilia asked. Lark was wondering the same thing.

"Southwestern New Mexico," Harry answered, uncrossing and recrossing his ankles. "However, it seems obvious Schottler's bird didn't know that."

Cecilia dug inside the heavy black leather purse she kept draped over her arm. "Wait. I have a guide book." She ran a finger down the index and flipped the book open to the photo plates. "Is this your bird?"

She held up the picture for Lark to see.

"That's it!"

"I'm telling you, it can't be," said Henderson, cramming another egg roll into his mouth. "Did anyone besides you and Rachel see this bird?"

Lark winced. She knew where this was going. Rachel was a novice birder. Her corroboration wouldn't satisfy anyone. "No."

He flung open his arms. "There you have it."

Lark ignored him. "I still want to know what the book says."

Cecilia skipped to the next page and scanned the text. "Found in Mexico and Central America in pine-oak forests. Reaches northern limit of range in Arizona and New Mexico." She glanced up, said, "Not exactly true," then glanced back down.

"Usually seen in mountain canyons at six thousand five hundred to nine thousand feet elevation. It prefers yellow pine, spruce, or Douglas fir and is often sighted near streams."

"Where did you say you spotted it?" Eric asked.

"On the peninsula."

"There are lots of pine trees on the peninsula, and it's near the stream's inlet," Cecilia said. "Plus Elk Park falls within the right zone, just a skosh north."

"Wishful thinking, if I ever heard it." Andrew spoke around a mouthful of egg rolls.

"It's been so hot, maybe the bird thought he was in New Mexico," countered Lark. "All I know is, I saw it, and it looked like that." She jabbed a finger at the guide book picture.

"You know," Harry said, straightening up. "Lark may be onto something."

"What? With the weather theory?" Eric asked, taking a swig of beer and winking at Lark.

Harry nodded. "With global warming, ecosystems change, and the creatures inhabiting those ecosystems change. Sometimes it happens over long periods of time; sometimes it occurs overnight."

Lark perked up. "You mean like what happened after the Mount Saint Helens eruption."

"Sure, that would be an example of a rapid occurrence."

Cecilia looked confused.

"I read about it in Audubon," explained Lark. "During the volcanic eruption, the pyroclastic flow sterilized the land around a place called Spirit Lake. It created an area called the Pumice Plain. Ten years after the blast, Forest Service ecologists started observing strange combinations of birds showing up in the area—birds associated, with more desert-like conditions. Like what you'd find in the Great Basin, rather than somewhere like the Cascade Range."

Lark glanced at Harry. He was nodding in agreement.

"Within five years," she continued, "the Plain was luring homed larks, American pipits, rock wrens, sparrows, meadowlarks, et cetera. And closer to the lake, where owls and osprey used to hunt, they were spotting red-winged blackbirds and spotted sandpipers."

Andrew snorted. "That said, we haven't had any drastic changes around here. Not since the Big Thompson flooded."

"Are you going to deny that it's been getting drier and drier every year?" Harry asked.

"No, but we're in a drought period."

"What about average temperatures? Don't you see them rising year after year?"

"Maybe in minute increments," conceded Andrew. "But, without a study, there's no way to know for sure."

"But there was a study done," Harry said. "It was published in the Journal of the Colorado Field Ornithologists. If I remember correctly, the author concluded that even a relatively small change in average temperature could impact bird distribution and affect ranges."

"Paraphrased nicely, but I'd have to read the article before—"

Several sharp taps on the podium microphone interrupted their conversation.

"—I could accept the theory," finished Andrew in a loud whisper.

"Try the July 2000 issue."

Paul Owens stepped up to the microphone, pulling Katherine with him. Dressed in matching khakis and ptarmigan-logoed T-shirts, they still managed to look mismatched. Next to Katherine, Paul looked tall. He was blond, boyishly handsome, and sparkled with energy and enthusiasm. Dark-haired and petite, Katherine's aloof manner increased her stature. And she looked out of place in silk-screened cotton.

"Hello, everyone," Paul said. "May I have your attention for just a few minutes. I'd like to make some introductions, then I'll let you go back to your conversations." He cleared his throat and leaned into the microphone. "First, I'd like to thank you all for being here. This is the best turnout ever."

The crowd applauded. Owens bobbed his head like a water duck.

"Second, I'd like to introduce you to my partner, Katherine Saunders."

There was another burst of applause, but this time Owens raised his hands for quiet.

"Katherine is a remarkable lady. An outstanding birder, a founding member, and a large financial supporter of the Migration Alliance. Without Katherine, MA wouldn't exist as we know it today."

"He could have trimmed that statement," murmured Dorothy, slipping up beside Lark.

"And ended with exist?" Lark asked.

Dorothy nodded.

Several others shushed them, as Katherine waved her hand side-to-side in the air. "Thank you, Paul. Everyone. It's so nice to be here."

Owens waited for the clapping to die down, basking in his partner's glory. "There are several other people I'd like to introduce, so if you could please hold your applause until the end…?" He consulted a stack of three-by-five cards he held in his hand, then looked up and smiled. "We're quite fortunate to have with us Buzz Aldefer, a major in the United States Air Force. Where are you, Buzz?"

A large man with graying sideburns and a buzz cut stepped out of the crowd and strode to the podium. Lark remembered seeing him the night before in the Drummond lounge.

"It's an honor to be here," Buzz said, his voice low and gravelly. He bent toward the microphone, stiffly from the waist.

"Buzz is but one of three military officers assigned to the Migration Alliance board, all of whom work primarily in a research capacity. By virtue of the fact that all three branches of the U.S. military participate in Migration Alliance, it becomes imminently clear the U.S. military understands the importance of defining the patterns of migratory birds."

"That's right, Paul. We feel that the greater our knowledge, the greater the assurance that neither our pilots nor the migrating birds shall meet with disaster during Air Force maneuvers or training exercises. Through our participation with MA, we clearly demonstrate our concern with the welfare of our nation and the welfare of the global environment."

Aldefer stepped away from the podium to a halfhearted round

of applause, clearly in violation of Paul's earlier instructions and clearly criticized by the majority of MA members.

"Thank you, Buzz." Paul clapped his hands near the mic, adding to the noise. Consulting his notes again, he said, "Next, I'd like to introduce someone who's here representing the coffee industry. Please welcome Jan Halloway."

Lark had seen her before, at the Warbler Café and in the lounge the night before. Dressed in blue jeans and a cardigan, she appeared altered from the image of power suits portrayed in the trade journals. Lark had been following her rise to power. She'd gone from steno pool to chief executive officer in under four years, becoming one of the country's youngest and highest-paid corporate CEOs. Her accomplishments elevated her in Lark's eyes, but in reality, it was a pair of two-inch platform heels that made her appear so tall. And she looked nervous, which didn't make sense. Halloway must have spoken in front of this many people hundreds of times.

"Good evening," said Halloway, stepping up to the podium. "Paul asked me to tell you about myself." She flashed a Pearl Drops smile and pushed back her streaked blond bangs. "I'm the CEO of Jitters Coffee Company. Have all of you heard of us?"

A hum rose from the crowd. A sea of heads bobbed.

"Then you know we are a franchise corporation that donates hundreds of thousands of dollars to the less-fortunate countries where we purchase our coffee supplies. The money is primarily used to educate farmers on the benefits of growing bird-supportive coffee, toward child education programs, and toward social development programs in a number of underdeveloped countries."

"Big whoopee," whispered Dorothy. She'd joined them after the speeches began and now stood with a sour look and her arms crossed. "Jitters' profits topped fourteen million per quarter last year. Their total revenue topped one billion. A few hundred thousand dollars…" She shook her head. "It's a drop in the bucket to them."

Lark calculated the amount in her head and came up with a number around 1 percent.

"Our interest," continued Halloway, "is in insuring our coffees are organically produced. That requires coffee be grown in shade, which, in turn, provides more and more treed habitat for birds. A win-win situation." She flashed another smile and waited for a spontaneous burst of applause to die down before gesturing toward a young Hispanic man hanging in the shadows. "Now, I'd like to introduce you to another member of our team. Someone who's worked for us for a while, but someone I've only met here, for the first time: Norberto Rincon. Step out here, Norberto." She stretched out a hand. A young man stepped out of the shadows and inched forward. Thin and wiry, he stood eye to eye with Jan and looked more wary than nervous.

A crash near the door caused him to spring backward and fade from sight. Lark stood on her tiptoes, straining to see what had happened. Buzz Aldefer was bent over, plucking splinters of glass off the patio floor.

Jan cleared her throat. "Norberto is Jitters' new middleman in Chiapas, Mexico, and a little shy. But he knows his business. Norberto serves as the go-between for the coffee bean growers and the Jitters Coffee Company. It's his job to arrange for the sale and delivery of all of our Mexican coffees."

"That's the canned version," whispered Dorothy, as Halloway stepped down.

Lark glanced at her sharply.

"All right, hold on, everyone," said Owens, applauding as he reclaimed the mic. "I have one more announcement to make." He bowed his head, then lifted his face slowly, his smile gone. "As some of you may have heard, Esther Mills, a longtime friend and expert birder, was murdered last night outside the Warbler Café."

A gasp tore through the crowd.

"Oh great," mumbled Lark. "That should do wonders for business."

One on either side of her, Cecilia and Dorothy both elbowed her in the ribs. "Shhh."

"Esther's death is a great loss to the birding community," continued Owens. "Dedicated to the preservation of bird habitat, she had devoted the last several years of her life to developing the Chipe Coffee Company, a company that purchased only hand-selected, organic coffees directly from Mexican coffee growers. The coffee beans, grown in pesticide-free, shade environments, were hand-delivered to warehouses in Denver, then resold and distributed through outlets up and down the Front Range. She was even looking into expanding her operation."

Really? thought Lark. If that was the case, why had Esther recently canceled all coffee deliveries until further notice?

Owens tossed his head, flipping back a lock of gold hair. "Esther was scheduled to speak during this year's conference. I've been informed that her business partner, Lark Drummond, one of Elk Park's local experts, has graciously offered to fill her place."

Lark felt the color drain from her face. She, give a speech? Lark turned to Dorothy, figuring that's who'd "graciously" volunteered her. Dorothy had disappeared. Smart woman.

"It came up suddenly," explained Cecilia nervously. "She was forced to make a command decision. She didn't think you'd mind."

"Well she should think again."

Owens craned his neck. "If you're here, Lark, raise your hand."

Dorothy had reappeared next to Owens and whispered in his ear, pointing in her direction.

"Oh, yes, I see her. She's way in the back, folks, close to the bar. Come on, Lark, put it up there so everyone can see who you are."

Lark forced a smile, made a silent promise to kill Dorothy, then slowly lifted her arm. The birders cheered.

Owens waited for the crowd to quiet. "For those of you who knew Esther, there will be a memorial service held in her honor Saturday afternoon. The time and location are posted on the bulletin board near the registration table."

A murmur swept the crowd as birders consulted their field trip schedules and conferred with one another.

Owens rapped his knuckles against the podium and consulted

his notes. "Hold onto your binoculars, I'm almost finished."

The crowd tittered.

"This next piece of news is a tad premature to announce, but I wanted all of you to be among the first to hear it. A little bird told me that Migration Alliance has been named the beneficiary of Esther's estate."

Lark frowned. Gil Arquette had told her Owens was the beneficiary and, therefore, one of her new partners. So why had Owens just announced the Migration Alliance as the beneficiary? Had she gotten the facts wrong? Had Arquette meant the Alliance, and mentioned Owens's name because he was MA's executive director? Or did Owens for some reason want people to think that the Alliance was the beneficiary and not him?

Chapter 8

Situated on the east end of town, the municipal building housed the mayor's offices, local planning and zoning offices, and the Elk Park Police Department. A nondescript gray, the two-story building, comprised of brick and mortar, stood back from the street and shared its parking lot with the public library. Parking spaces unoccupied by town personnel were generally occupied by tourists choosing to ignore the Municipal Building and Library Parking Only—All Other Vehicles Will Be Towed signs. Today was no exception.

Lark weaved through the parking lot twice, then jimmied her truck into a one-hour parking slot on the street. Cracking her windows against the heat, she snatched the field notebook she'd picked up at Bird Haven off the seat, and sprinted for the building.

The sergeant at the desk waved her through, pointing her to an office in the corner. Bernie sat behind a gray desk, feet propped up, reading the Elk Park Gazette.

"Anything interesting?"

"Speculation about Esther's murder." He set the paper down on his desk and tapped the front page. "They're reporting it as a robbery run amok." He gestured to a gray chair the color of the building, the walls, and the carpet. The only color in the room was on Bernie. He wore a bright blue T-shirt tucked into gray regulation trousers. "Have a seat."

Lark sidled into the room. "I came for the keys and to give you this." She waved the field notebook.

Bernie leaned over the desk and dangled a ring of keys on the tip of his index finger. "I'll trade ya."

Lark hesitated, then took the keys and handed over the notebook. "I'd like it back."

Bernie shrugged. "First, let's have a look-see."

"Check out the last page." Lark pocketed the keys. "Like I think I told you, I was calling out marks on the bird, when I sighted the murder taking place. I guess I just kept calling out things, because Rachel wrote down the letters, 'black mask' and 'gloves.'"

"EZLN." Crandall scrunched up his face and scratched his head. "Any idea what it means?"

Lark shook her head. "Not a clue."

"Okay. I'll look into it." He snapped the notebook shut. Lark reached for it, but Bernie held it away. "I think I'll hang onto this for a while."

"Of course you will."

Bernie grinned. "You look like hell, Drummond."

Lark made a face. "Thanks. Just what a girl likes to hear in the morning."

It didn't help that he was right. Last night's lack of sleep fretting over her new partnership with Owens had taken its toll. She'd tried washing away the telltale bags, but to no avail. Leave it to Bernie to point it out. "Take it back or I won't tell you what else I know."

"Spill it."

"For some reason, Paul Owens is trying to cover up the fact that he, not the Alliance, inherited Esther's money."

That seemed to get Bernie's attention. He pinned her with his sharp blue gaze.

Lark filled him in on Owens' announcement at the kick-off bash. "Gil Arquette told me he had called Paul, so Paul knew the money was left to him. Instead, he announced that it was bequeathed to the Migration Alliance."

"So?"

"So, obviously he wants everyone to think Esther left the money to the Alliance, not him. Why? Unless he's trying to cover up something."

Bernie leaned back, draped his arms over his head, and stared thoughtfully into space. "You know, Drummond. You may actually have something there."

Lark's next stop was the Warbler Café. Out of morbid curiosity, she parked in the back lot and crossed the pavement. Halfway to the back door, she found the dark stain. In spite of the officer's hosing, blood remained. The sun beat down, baking it into the hot asphalt. She hurried to the back door and turned the key.

By contrast, the Warbler was dark and cool. Lark shivered, rubbing her arms. She'd come to believe that the spirits of those who died violently sometimes lingered, either out of disbelief and shock or to insure that justice be done before the spirit moved on.

Esther clung to the Warbler. In the furnishings, in the paintings, in the very essence of the building, she remained. Lark whispered a promise to help find her killer and then, with a flick of the light switch, dispelled the shadows and made a beeline for the office.

She spent the morning poring over the books, perusing work schedules, payroll information, and accessory supply sheets. In a ledger detailing shipments and purchases, Lark found some odd numbers scribbled on several pages. From what she could decipher, it seemed Esther tracked all shipments out of Chiapas, not just the ones she made. And the numbers were staggering.

Toward the back of the ledger, Lark found what she was looking for: an inventory record. According to the numbers, coffee on site posed no problem, but warehouse supplies appeared to be running low.

Lark dialed the number on the warehouse inventory list and spoke with someone in the billing department of Commercial Storage.

"I don't know anything about any coffee supply," explained the woman in nasal tones. "The way we work things, you pay us for warehouse space, and we give you a password to the main gate and keys to the warehouse at one of our five locations. But, honey, unless you can prove you're the person who signed the contracts, that's all the information you get."

Lark thanked her, then hung up and rummaged through the filing cabinets for a folder containing the code to the warehouse. The key had to be one of those dangling from the key ring Bernie had given her, but it would be totally useless without the password to the main gate.

The code turned up in a file marked "Storage." The warehouse address was listed as Lyons, somewhere off of Highway 7 and U.S. 36. Lark started a new to-do list: "Check warehouse."

On a hunch, she picked up the phone and dialed the Drummond.

"Stephen?"

"Lark, thank heavens."

"Stephen, I need to know who distributes coffee for the Chipe Coffee Company."

"Where are you?"

None of your business. "I'm at the Warbler, and I need to know who delivers Chipe's coffee to the Drummond." She spoke slowly, enunciating each word, hoping he would take the hint and just answer her question. "Off the top of your head, do you remember the name of the delivery company? Or can you look it up in the orders for me?" She paused, then added "please" as an afterthought.

"When are you coming back?"

She heard the rustling of papers. "Are you searching through the invoices?"

"You haven't forgotten we have the Migration Alliance banquet this evening?"

"No, I haven't forgotten, Stephen." Lark sucked in a breath, annoyed by his persistence. "I'm sure you're dealing with things just fine. Now, did you find the information?"

Velof sighed. "The company is Talley Distributing."

"Do you have a phone number?"

He rattled off ten digits, and she hung up before he could harangue her anymore. Knowing Velof, he'd still have plenty to say later this afternoon.

The clerk at Talley Distributing connected her with the shipping manager, who connected her with the supervisor, who connected her with Mr. Talley.

"What exactly do you want?" he demanded.

"I'm looking for an explanation as to why Esther Mills canceled Chipe Coffee Company's Wednesday-afternoon deliveries. From the inventory sheets, it appears that the coffee supply, though dwindling, is still adequate for filling orders."

"Why don't you ask her?" he replied. "I can't hardly wait to talk to her myself."

Didn't he know? "I hate to be the bearer of bad news, Mr.

Talley, but Esther Mills is dead."

He choked and sputtered into the phone. "Come again?"

"She was murdered two days ago. Shortly after she canceled the deliveries."

"You're shittin' me."

"No."

Talley let out a long, low whistle. "Hey, you're not accusing me of doin' nothing, are you?"

"No, I'm just trying to figure out what's going on with Chipe Coffee Company."

There was a long silence, then Talley said, "According to my boys, Mills had no good reason to cancel out. Not unless she was looking for a way to stick it to me."

"Is there a reason she'd want to do that?"

"None that I know of, but she was a strange bird." Talley cleared his throat. "How 'bout I offer you a proposition?"

Business or personal? "I'm listening."

"Esther owes a twenty-five percent cancellation fee for Wednesday. It's legal-like, all part of the contract. But how 'bout, I'll waive the fee if you go ahead and authorize me and the boys to deliver the goods as scheduled. We can fill the orders this coming Wednesday, one week late. What do you say?"

Lark scrunched her eyes closed and let out a sigh. What could she say? "That's a generous offer, Mr. Talley."

"Darn tootin'. Of course, it isn't every day somebody kicks the bucket. Consider it a favor to you."

Lark weighed the options. She could sit on the delivery, which forced Chipe Coffee Company customers up and down the Front Range to find another distributor, or she could accept the man's offer.

"Mr. Talley, you have a deal."

Lark hung up, pushing the phone away, hoping she'd made the right decision and that there wasn't some special reason Esther'd postponed delivery of the coffee supply. If so, it was too late now.

The next order of business was finding Esther's speech.

Replacing the file on the warehouse, she thumbed through the remaining folders. Knowing Esther, she'd made handwritten notes. So where were they stashed?

Lark searched the desk, then the credenza, and turned up nothing. At that point, she checked the computer. There were no files that indicated Esther'd been working on anything, and the disks in the disk holder were all clearly marked with what was on them. Esther must have been working on the speech at home.

Esther's house was located twelve miles outside of town. The cabin—a small, two-bedroom log home, chinked together with white grout—had belonged to Esther's grandmother, Paris. The house looked the same as it always had, but Esther had added her own unique touches to the surrounding acreage. In back, she'd built a giant labyrinth bordered in wildflowers. A pair of bronzed lions flanked the driveway entrance. Sundials and bluebird houses dotted the yard. Beneath the windows, fresh herbs cascaded from whitewashed window boxes.

Lark climbed out of the truck. Visiting Esther's was like stepping back in time to the sixties or forward into a New Age Mecca. She found it hard to see how Victor Garcia, a thirty-year law enforcement veteran and straight-nosed cop, fit in.

"Vic?" Lark tapped on the front door. She heard the scrape of a chair.

"What do you want?" He came to the door in wrinkled clothes, with a three-day's growth of beard on his face. His eyes looked bloodshot, and Lark smelled whiskey on his breath.

"Not doing so good?"

He rolled his eyes and stumbled back inside. Lark followed him into the kitchen. A half-full glass sat in the middle of a small wooden table beside a half-empty bottle of whiskey. Another empty bottle lay on the floor beside the chair. A thin layer of dust coated the counters, making it clear no one had used the kitchen in days.

"Have you eaten anything, Vic?"

"Nah. I'm not hungry. This is all I need." He held up the bottle and took a deep swig.

"Yeah? Well, I don't agree." Lark snatched up the rag draped over the faucet, wet it, and wiped down the counter. Crossing to the refrigerator, she pulled out a carton of eggs and flipped the stove on. "You have to eat something, Vic. You have a funeral to plan."

He snapped back in the chair as though she'd stuck him, then buried his head in his arms on the table. "I can't bury her."

"So we'll have a memorial service and you can scatter the ashes."

"I can't scatter the ashes, either."

Lark thought of Cecilia's story and shuddered. "What are you planning to do, then? Keep the ashes on the mantel?"

"I don't even have a mantel," he said with a bitter edge to his voice. "Didn't you hear? She left everything to that Migration Alliance dude."

"I heard."

"Even the frickin' house."

She hadn't realized that Owens got the property, too. That didn't seem fair. And it didn't seem like something Esther would do. "Who told you Owens got everything?"

"Bernie Crandall. He said he was convinced I killed her, except he was having trouble finding a motive."

"Maybe there's been a mistake."

"Hah. Fat chance." Vic took another swig from the bottle.

"You can't be sure of that. You two were living together like husband and wife. Maybe that makes you her common law husband?"

Vic's head came up. "It might, huh?"

"Yeah." Lark nodded, pleased that she might have found a solution to Vic's problem. "If so, you're entitled to some of the estate. If I were you, I'd check with Gil Arquette."

"I'll do just that," said Vic, scraping back his chair and staggering to his feet.

"Later," ordered Lark, pushing him back down on the seat. "Right now, you're going to eat something. And give me that." She took the bottle away from him and, against his protests, poured the contents down the sink.

Two eggs, some bacon, and several stiff cups of coffee

restored Vic to some semblance of the man Lark knew. After she explained what she was looking for, he pointed her to a rolltop desk in the living room.

"How about I take a look while you go shower?" she suggested, clearing the dishes to the sink. "Then we can talk about what we're doing on Saturday."

A shadow crossed his face at the thought. "I can't let go."

Feeling helpless, Lark patted his shoulder. "We'll work on it together."

She waited until he'd disappeared into the bedroom before rolling up the desk's top and rifling the contents of Esther's desk. The sight might have been more than he could handle.

The pigeonholes were full of treasures: old fountain pens, wax and wax stamps, tissue writing paper. In one cubbyhole on the right, she found a stack of letters. Most of the postmarks were old, dated from the 1920s, and showed Paris Mills' address on the return. One or two were more recent.

Curiosity prompted Lark to open one postmarked two years ago from Mexico. It read:

My dearest Esther,

Though it's been only one day since you've been gone, in my heart it feels like months, years, an eternity. Knowing we may never be together again makes it all the harder.

Katherine returns today…

Katherine? Lark flipped to the last page and looked for the signature.

Yours forever and ever, Paul

Paul Owens. It had to be. The stamp was Mexican, and the postmark read San Cristóbal de las Casas. That was one of the places Esther bought coffee in Chiapas.

Esther Mills had been having an affair with Paul Owens. So that's what he had been covering up. Lark wondered if Vic knew. Esther was the love of his life. If he had discovered she carried a torch for another man, might he have been jealous enough to kill her? More likely, he'd have killed Owens.

And what about Katherine? Even though she and Paul weren't married, she seemed very possessive of her partner.

The sound of the closet door clicking into place prompted Lark to put the letter back in its envelope. But instead of sticking it back into its pigeonhole, she crammed it into her pocket

"Find what you were looking for?"

Lark glanced up. Vic stood in the doorway, shaved and wearing clean clothes. His eyes looked tired but alert. "Not yet," she said.

"What are these?" He walked over and reached toward the letters. Lark held up a hand, but he plucked a stack of three-by-five cards from the next pigeonhole.

Lark's heart pounded as she flipped through the stack. "Blank index cards." She shoved them back in the desk. "It must not be here."

"I saw her working on it."

At Vic's insistence, Lark searched the desk again. Nothing turned up.

"Do you have a computer?"

"Not at home. We don't even have a TV out here at the house. Esther thought the radiation off the screens was dangerous. She even avoided using the computer she had at work."

That fit with the earth mother image, thought Lark. Then another idea flickered through her mind. The speech was obviously missing. Vic had seen her working on it Maybe it had been stolen. Maybe Esther was killed not for money as they initially thought but for something she knew. Something she had planned to reveal.

Chapter 9

Teresa Cruz was waiting on the front steps of the carriage house when Lark returned, and she followed Lark into the house.

"I need to talk to you," she said.

"About what?" Lark tossed the truck keys onto the counter, along with the ledger she'd brought home from the Warbler. She wanted to look more closely at the figures posted inside that didn't make sense. Dates and numbers—large numbers—reflecting purchases and sales too large for Esther to have made.

"I want to know what is happening with my immigration." The expression on Teresa's face read trouble.

Lark puffed her bangs back, picked up the Migration Alliance schedule, and turned to face the girl. "Bottom line? It doesn't look good, Teresa."

"What do you mean?" The girl's eyes widened in fear. Dressed in a T-shirt, shorts, and flip-flops, she looked small and vulnerable. Lark felt sorry for her, but facts were facts.

"I spoke with the attorney," she said. "He's looking into alternatives, but there isn't much hope. He expects you'll be sent back to Mexico and that you'll have to resubmit an application for a permanent visa. The odds aren't in your favor."

"I can't go back. I won't."

Where had she heard that before? "I don't think you'll have a choice. Unless you have a special skill of some kind that you're keeping secret."

"Like what?" Hope resonated in Teresa's voice.

Lark rolled the program schedule and slapped it against her thigh. "Like you can play pro baseball or can rid the world of cancer."

"I can sing."

"It doesn't qualify. I asked." Lark started past her into the living room, but Teresa grabbed her arm. Her fingers bit into Lark's flesh.

"You don't have to turn me in," she cried. "If they don't catch me, then they don't know I'm not supposed to be here."

Hadn't Arquette suggested the same alternative? The consequences scared her, though. "And what happens if they do catch you? Then both our butts are in a sling."

Teresa shook her head, black hair flying. "No, because you don't know for sure that my visa's no good."

Lark gestured for the girl to sit down on the couch, then pulled up the easy chair opposite. "Teresa, I'd like to help you, but I don't know what I can do. If I hire you without a green card, I put my business in jeopardy. Same deal if I know your visa's expired and don't turn you in. But for the sake of argument, let's say I look the other way because I'm not sure. How are you going to live? Where are you going to get the money to support yourself?"

Teresa wet her lips. "If you give me a job, Peter says he'll take the blame if INS finds out."

"Great. Why doesn't he just marry you?" she mumbled.

"He offered." Teresa met Lark's gaze, then looked away, worrying her hands in her lap. "I can't. I don't want to."

Lark asked herself whether she really wanted to know the reason, then curiosity got the better of her. "Why?"

"Because I'm already married." Teresa's chin jutted up defiantly.

Lark stared at the girl, then leaned back in her chair, stunned. "Married?"

Teresa nodded.

You're just a baby. "Where is your husband?"

"He's still in Mexico."

Lark closed her eyes and rested her head against the chair. This whole thing was getting more and more convoluted. "Care to tell me what happened?"

Teresa stuck out her lip. "No."

Spoiled didn't begin to define this girl. "Then," Lark said, scooting to the edge of her chair, "I guess this conversation is over."

"Wait!" Teresa reached out her hand, preventing Lark from rising. A teardrop etched its way down her cheek. "I was sixteen when I met Jesus. We fell very much in love, and I married him…against my father's wishes."

Why didn't that surprise her ?

"My father, he told me Jesus was trouble, but I didn't believe him."

"Did your father say why he thought he was trouble?"

"I knew why. It's because he cares so much for the cause of the Zapatistas."

Lark frowned. "Jesus or your father?"

"Jesus." Teresa smiled, tears fell in glossy lines down her cheeks. "My father is a coffee farmer. He wants only to grow his crop and make the money to feed his family. He would do anything to take care of us. But not Jesus. He is a rebel, a freedom fighter. He wears the mask of the Zapatista with pride." She brushed the tears away with the back of her hand. "Do you remember what I told you about the PRI invading Las Abejas?"

"You spoke of women and children, of your mother, dying."

"Sí, murdered at the hands of the PRI and their La Mascara Roja. Jesus lost two sisters that day. He was very angry."

Lark drew a ragged breath. "I can understand why."

"He was determined to…how do you say?"

"Retaliate?"

"Sí. He and several of his friends sneaked in and attacked La Mascara Roja still guarding the area. One of the presidente's sons was assigned to the squad. He was killed in the attack, and my Jesus was blamed."

"So now he's wanted for murder," Lark said. An eye for an eye, until the last one dies.

"If they catch him, he will be executed."

Seeing the anguish on Teresa's face, Lark felt her own eyes tear. "I'm sorry."

Teresa pursed her lips. "The PRI knows I am married to Jesus. They came to my father's house looking for him the day Esther was there to buy coffee. They demanded to question me, but I was not home. My father, in fear for my life, found me and sent me away with Esther."

"And Jesus?" Lark almost hated to ask.

"He is safe, hiding in the mountains of Chiapas. Without me to give away his hiding place, he will never be caught. Until there is peace, he must wear his mask."

The image of someone in a black ski mask flashed through Lark's mind. "Teresa, what does a Zapatista mask look like? What color is it?"

Her eyes narrowed. "Black."

"Plain black?"

"Except for the signature of the Ejército Zapatista de Liberación Nacional."

"Spelled out like that?"

"No, spelled only in letters."

Ejèrcito Zapatista de Liberación Nacional. EZLN.

The Migration Alliance banquet was scheduled to start in the ballroom at seven. Cocktails were served on the Drummond patio beforehand, and there was a full crowd.

Shortly after Teresa's revelation, Velof had shown up demanding attention to last-minute details. Lark had promised to be there shortly, then sent Teresa back to the Manor House. The girl left grudgingly, but not before extracting a promise from Lark to consider her request to remain at the Drummond.

Once they were both gone, Lark tried calling Bernie and was forced to leave a message on his voicemail. Now, having refixed her hair in a French braid and decked herself out in a multicolored broomstick skirt with a lavender T-shirt and silver jewelry, Lark wanted a drink.

Before leaving the house, she browsed through the ledger again, trying to figure out what bothered her. Something in the numbers didn't fit. She started to set the ledger back on the counter, then changed her mind. Too easy to spill something on it. Crossing to the bookshelf, she slipped the ledger into a space between the Joy of Cooking and The Guide to Colorado Birds. That ought to keep it safe.

"You look nice," Eric Linenger said, squeezing in behind her at the bar. Lark had seen him come in and was secretly pleased when he'd made a beeline across the patio, past Nora Frank, his fellow ranger and wanna-be girlfriend, to find her. Nora didn't look happy. Lark smiled at him and ordered two beers.

"Flattery buys you a drink."

"Then I'll have to do it more often." He raised his bottle in a silent toast. "Though," he paused, looking at her seriously, "I did mean what I said."

Lark felt the blood rise to her cheeks. "Thanks." You don't look too bad yourself. Tipping her head back, she studied him. Tonight he was in uniform—khaki shorts, a short-sleeve shirt, and hiking boots—and he looked almost James Bond-ish in a pair of aviator sunglasses. His wind-tousled brown hair reached his collar, adding to the rakish look. She was about to say something, when she noticed Officer Klipp slip out through the patio doors. Stepping to one side, he pressed his back to the wall and scanned the crowd.

"You seem sort of distracted. Is something wrong?"

Klipp left, and Lark turned her attention back to Eric. "Have you got an hour?"

"That bad?"

"You don't know the half of it." Lark took a swig of beer.

"Try me."

"The question is, where to begin? Can you keep a secret?"

"On Scout's honor," he said, flashing the Boy Scout's salute.

First she told him about Teresa, about Teresa's connection to the Zapatistas, and about the emblem on the hat belonging to the masked killer, leaving out the part about the expired visa. Then she told him about her visit to Vic's, about the letter she found, and about the strange notes in the ledger. "Were you here when Paul Owens announced that the Migration Alliance may have been named in Esther's will?"

Eric nodded.

"It isn't the MA that inherited her percentage in Chipe Coffee Company. It was Owens himself."

Eric whistled. "So everything fits with the letter."

"That was my take on it." Lark held out the MA schedule of events. "Now, top things off with the fact that I have staff out with the flu. I'm scheduled to lead a half-day hike in the morning with no one available to replace me; Dorothy tried. Esther's memorial service is set for tomorrow afternoon. I lead an all-day hike on Sunday. Plus, I have to deliver Esther's speech on Thursday. With no notes, I might add. You might say

85

it's been a hell of a week already."

Eric draped his arm affectionately across her shoulders. "Whine, whine, whine. Be honest. You love the hikes."

"Oh, and I almost forgot," she said. "We're reopening the Warbler. Tomorrow, after the service."

"So soon?" Eric pulled his arm away. Lark masked her disappointment.

"We can't afford to keep it closed."

The call sounded for everyone to enter the ballroom, and the two of them moved in that direction. Eric pocketed his sunglasses, and they found two seats at one of the EPOCH tables. Andrew and Opal Henderson staked claim to another two chairs, and Gertie plopped down to save places for Harry, Dorothy, and Cecilia.

"What's on the menu tonight?" Andrew asked, folding his napkin into his lap.

"That depends on what you checked off on your registration," Lark replied. "I'm having the beef."

A variety of dishes were served, starting with salad and ending with chocolate mousse. As the last dessert was served, Paul Owens stood up and banged his spoon against his glass.

"Good evening. May I have everyone's attention? I think everyone has their desserts by now, so we'd like to get started with our program this evening."

The room quieted. Lark glanced around at the other guests. Some leaned forward with interest, while others dabbed at their mouths with their napkins and cast about for an avenue of escape. Lark's desire fell somewhere in between.

"So, let's get right to it." Owens smiled. "Tonight's speaker, Katherine Saunders, is someone I know quite well.

"An avid birder from the time she can remember. Her father, Preston Saunders, instilled in Katherine a love for all things avian. He became a birder when taxonomy was still considered a valid method for identifying birds, so Katherine grew up in a home filled with stuffed rarities. She learned quickly how to identify the species and took to photographing our feathered friends. It was the Saunders money that helped found the Migration Alliance, and that helps fund a variety of programs throughout the world geared toward the preservation and conservation of birds.

"So, without further ado, may I introduce my partner and colleague, Katherine Saunders."

The room thundered with applause. Katherine approached the podium and adjusted the mic. Short, with dark hair that flipped up on her shoulders, she wore a cream-colored suit and shoes to match her lime-green shirt.

"Good evening," she said in a lilting, birdlike voice. "I'm very happy to be here." She bowed her head, waited until the crowd quieted, then began. "It's midday in the mountains of Chiapas, Mexico, yet the sun works hard to penetrate the dense air. Is it clouds, fog, or smoke that chokes out the light, making it hard to determine the time of day?

"The smell of burning vegetation eddies around you. Someone is clearing land by burning away the trees and scrub.

"Up the road walks a farmer. He is headed to the village to eat lunch. He walks past scarred mountainsides and wonders why his neighbors still practice a method of coffee growing that requires the destruction of vegetation and brings death to the songbirds and creatures of the land.

"The farmer doesn't agree with the old way. Fires often burn out of control, destroying prime forests and habitat. Soil erosion is a major problem. No, this farmer is part of a pilot program sponsored by Migration Alliance to help train coffee growers in the techniques necessary to successfully cultivate organic, shade-grown coffee.

"In Mexico, coffee plantations account for seventy-five percent of the tropical habitat, providing homes for over one hundred twenty species of migratory birds." She allowed her words to sink in. "Yet, over the past ten years, forty percent of the coffee plantations have converted their operations to sun-grown production, resulting in a significant loss of habitat and a significant decline in the numbers of migratory birds. Songbirds are hit the hardest.."

Katherine leaned into the podium. "Since the 1970s, the number of coffee plants per hectare, the equivalent of two and half acres, has increased from eleven hundred to as high as seven thousand plants. Sun-based and high-yield, these plants require the use of petroleum-based fertilizers, herbicides, insecticides, and fungicides. And ninety percent fewer bird species live in this habitat." Katherine shuffled her note cards.

"So, the question becomes," she continued, "how to continue market expansion for the coffee industry and still promote forest conservation and environmental quality critical for the migratory birds?" She looked up and grinned. "I can hear some of you asking, 'Why worry about the coffee industry?'"

The crowd laughed. Several pushed away their coffee cups, obviously willing to sacrifice a cup of java for the avian population.

"I'll tell you why. Because it's a five billion dollar industry, that's why. An industry that provides work for over three million Mexican citizens." Katherine paused, searching the faces of her listeners. "And I'll tell you how: By working with Mexico and the other coffee-growing countries to promote coffee production in shade environments, either by offering incentives or by forcing compliance to new regulations imposed by their governments, at MA's urging."

Katherine went on to explain the Smithsonian Migratory Bird Center's Shade Management Criteria for Bird-Friendly Coffee. According to her, the SMBC acknowledged only two types of shade: rustic shade and planted shade.

"Rustic shade consists of natural forest vegetation," Katherine explained. "If additional trees have been planted, the system is then called a traditional polyculture. And even in this type of system, trees are generally thinned and trimmed to reduce undergrowth and overgrowth in hopes of increasing light. The SMBC recommends that a minimum canopy cover of forty percent be maintained.

"A planted shade environment contains a backbone of trees, such as Inga and Erythrina, that provides the optimal shade environment for the coffee plant. And, as the diversity of trees in the plantation increases, so does the number of species of birds. In fact, probably more critical for avian diversity is the stature of the trees. The backbone shade species must be allowed to attain twelve to fifteen meters in height."

Katherine tucked a loose strand of hair behind her ear. "But shade alone is not enough. MA must push for organic designation. Current national crop production standards requirements for organic labeling read that the agricultural products must 'not be produced on land to which any prohibited substances, including synthetic chemicals, have been applied during the three years immediately preceding the harvest of the agricultural products.'"

Katherine looked up from her note cards, scanned the room, and held up two fingers. "Currently, only one to two percent of the coffee produced in the world qualifies. Of the five million bags of coffee produced in Mexico last year, only sixty thousand qualified to be tagged as organic." She shook her head.

"So, now you ask, how is the Migration Alliance working to help maintain, improve, and increase bird habitat in Mexico? Well, I'll tell you." Katherine punched her fist on the podium, and Lark jumped, along with everyone else at her table. "By teaching the farmers. MA supports a team of agronomists who make village visits, supervising, monitoring, and teaching farmers methods of terracing, composting, pruning, and intercropping plants for shade diversity."

She lowered her head again. "Consumers, we must unite." Her voice crescendoed as she spoke. "We must purchase only organic coffee from legitimate distributors, and we must do it now, for the sake of the birds. For the sake of humanity."

Katherine stepped back from the podium and the crowd roared to life. Several people stamped their feet and whistled.

A waiter approached Lark on the right. "Do you care for some coffee, ma'am?"

"Is it organic?" Gertie asked, a smug look on her face.

"As a matter of fact, yes," Lark replied. "That's all we serve."

"Good for you," Andrew said. "In that case, pour me one, too."

The waiter poured coffee all around. Lark had barely taken a sip when Velof appeared in the doorway and set a course in her direction.

"Here comes trouble," Eric said softly.

Velof scooted between the tables, apologizing to people he

89

bumped into along the way. He stopped opposite Lark, standing directly behind Dorothy. "May I speak with you, please?"

"Can't it wait?" Lark asked, setting down her coffee cup.

"No!" Velof exclaimed. "Bernie Crandall is in your office demanding to see Teresa Cruz. Wouldn't you know, the girl has disappeared."

Chapter 10

Lark found Bernie Crandall sitting behind her desk, bouncing an eraser off the desk blotter.

"So where's the girl, Drummond?"

"How should I know?" Lark said. "Your guess is as good as mine."

Crandall palmed the eraser, leaned back, and put his feet up on the desk. "You saw her last."

"Correction," Lark said, batting his feet to the floor. "Stephen saw her last."

Crandall straightened and started bouncing the eraser again. "Okay, I'll give you that. But he says he walked her back to the Manor House about two o'clock in the afternoon, and she seemed real upset over some conversation she'd had with you. Care to elaborate for me?"

Lark chewed on her lower lip. Part of her wanted to protect the girl; the other part questioned the wisdom of covering up for a possible killer. Self-preservation finally forced her to come clean. "Look, she's in the States on an expired visa. Gil Arquette was trying to wangle an extension, but things weren't looking real promising. I had just told her, when Stephen popped in all hot over the fact that I'd been out all morning when he needed help making decisions for the banquet tonight."

"For what it's worth, it looked to me like things went off without a hitch."

"Finally, a break."

"I know what you mean." Crandall unfolded himself from the chair, stretching as he stood. "I could sure use one."

Lark wet her lips. "Then I guess I'll tell you. I know what the letters on the mask stand for."

"You do? What?"

"The Ejército Zapatista de Liberación Nacional."

"Which means?"

"It's the name for an organization of freedom fighters operating in southern Mexico made up of Mexican Indians called the Zapatistas."

91

"Who told you this, Drummond?"

"Teresa." She filled him in on their conversation.

"Interesting." Crandall scratched his jaw. "Look, Drummond, I need to talk to the girl. If you see her again, I expect you to hang onto her and touch base with me."

"You'll be the first one I call."

After six hours of sleep and a quick shower, Lark pulled on a clean pair of shorts, a fuchsia-colored T-shirt, matching socks, and her hiking boots. Grabbing her birding gear and a jacket, she snagged a chocolate doughnut and a cup of coffee off the continental breakfast buffet on her way through the Drummond and scooted out the side door of the hotel, plopping down in a chair on the west end veranda.

"Are you our leader?" asked a bright-eyed woman in a mesh birding vest.

"That's me."

"I'll go tell the others you're here." The woman scurried off toward a group of about fifteen birders gathered near a large white bus. A sign reading Endovalley was taped to the inside of the windshield glass.

Assignments for the birding field trips had been dished out on a first-come, first-served basis to leaders and participants alike, and Lark had switched hers to a half-day trip. Originally, she'd been scheduled to lead the Pawnee National Grassland tour. But like the other groups going to Arapaho National Wildlife Refuge and Tamarack Ranch, the Pawnee tour was a full-day trip. Lark needed to be back for the two-thirty memorial service.

"There you are," Dorothy said, charging across the parking lot in a pink birding cap. She clutched white name badges and species cards in hand. "I brought you a new name tag. I figured you would misplace your other one."

Lark reluctantly pinned the badge on her shirt pocket. Not quite as bad as the bright yellow bus tags with school name and phone number that she'd been forced to wear in third grade, but close. She took another bite of her doughnut. "Where are you going today?"

"I'm in charge of the alpine tundra trip. Ptarmigans and brown-capped rosy-finches." Dorothy consulted her clipboard, flipping to a second set of pages. "You're in charge of the Endovalley. Three-toed woodpeckers, preferably nesting."

The area loosely called the Endovalley covered a relatively small section of the park just west of the Alluvial Fan. In actuality, it was a picnic area at the end of the Endovalley Road, approximately two miles off Highway 34.

The Alluvial Fan was all the evidence that remained of the Flood of 1982, when the earthen dam at Lawn Lake failed, pouring 674 acre-feet of water down the steep drainage of the Roaring River. A wall of water reached thirty-foot heights in the narrows, cutting a deep gash in the ground, dislodging hundreds of boulders, uprooting trees, and washing away the soil. The destructive force of the flood was immense. Three campers lost their lives. Millions of dollars in damage resulted. Horseshoe Park became a temporary lake, and Elk Park stood hip deep in muddy water. But the dead trees in the Fan area provided great habitat for viewing swallows, sapsuckers, flickers, and hairy woodpeckers.

Dorothy smoothed the pages on the clipboard. "You've been assigned bus number thirteen. You should have about forty birders. There's a cooler of water in the back…" She glanced at Lark over the top of her reading glasses. "In case anyone forgot to bring a water bottle."

"Mine's in my backpack, Dorothy."

"And there's sunscreen, bug spray, and a first-aid kit. There are also several large cartons of boxed lunches in the cargo area."

By now, ten or twelve of the gathered birders had crowded around, and Lark began assessing her group. There were a couple of novice birders, evidenced by the lack of equipment and preparedness, and several veterans, who she knew were probably better qualified to lead this trip than she was. The face in the crowd that intrigued her the most was that of Norberto Rincon.

"Gather round, folks," Dorothy called out. "This is Lark Drummond, and she will be your leader today." In a softer voice, she whispered, "Good luck. Sorry I couldn't find anyone to take your spot. I'll meet you back here at one-thirty."

"Thanks, Dee." Lark pushed herself up from the seat and smiled. "Good morning, everyone."

Silence.

"Okay. First off, I see some of you don't have jackets. This is Elk Park, and we are going to be climbing a bit in altitude, birding at elevations around 8,500 to 9,000 feet. I'd advise you to take the time to go back to your rooms and grab something. It's been unseasonably warm, but you never know when a storm might roll in."

No one made a move, so she continued.

"Okay, then general info time. The Endovalley covers multiple habitats. We can expect to see a lot of birds this morning, everything from western wood-pewee to rock wren. Is there anything in particular anyone's dying to see?"

"It's all new to me," said a heavyset woman dressed in heavily pocketed camouflage. A pair of Leica binoculars were draped around her neck, indicating she'd bought the best of everything to embark on this new adventure. A brand-new guidebook protruded from one of her front pockets. A water bottle bulged from the other.

"I could use a western tanager for my life list," responded a younger man wearing jeans and a Migration Alliance T-shirt. His name badge tagged him as Art.

"What's a life list?" the woman in camouflage asked. She flashed her badge at Lark. Her name was Molly.

Art rolled his eyes.

"A life list is a list that a birder keeps of all the birds he or she ever spots," Lark patiently explained. She handed the woman a species card, then passed one to each of the birders. "This card lists only the birds of our area, while a life list covers the world."

"Don't you think it's about time to get going?" Art demanded.

Lark tarried long enough to make him antsy, then loaded the bird-watchers into the bus and instructed the driver to stop at Endovalley picnic area.

Passing Elk Lake on the ride up, they snagged a Canada goose and several mallards, as well as a red-tailed hawk hunting along the road.

"Listen up, folks," Lark said when they crossed the bridge at Roaring River.

"American dipper on the left," someone from the back of the bus called out.

"Where?" Molly cried, struggling to find her binoculars among her other paraphernalia.

"It's gone now," Art said. "It went under the bridge."

Lark noted the disappointment on Molly's face and stood up, addressing the group as a whole. "Everyone will have another chance at the dipper. We're going to start at the end of the road, at the Endovalley picnic area, work our way back to this point, and eat lunch at the picnic area we're passing on the right."

Gazing out the window, Molly waved her hand in the air. "What happened here? Was there a fire?"

"Flood." Lark filled them in on some of the history of the area as they drove along. "Up here on the left, you'll see a historical marker. This is the Convicts' Cabin site, where convicts were housed to help build the Old Fall River Road in 1913.

"I'm sure you've all noticed how varied the habitat is in through here," she continued. "Near the Alluvial Fan there are lots of dead trees and tree cavities, home to a population of birds: swallows, sapsuckers, flickers, and hairy woodpeckers. Along the lake, you can see spotted sandpipers. And, in the willows along Fall River, you find hummingbirds and warblers."

The bus pulled into the Endovalley parking lot and circled around the one-way drive, stopping in front of the compost outhouses. Picnic tables were scattered beside willow-choked wetlands, and on either side of the river lay mixed forests of lodgepole pine, Engelmann spruce, Douglas fir, and aspen.

Lark consulted her watch. "Okay, folks, it's six-thirty now. This is the place for a pit stop. We'll bird this area for a while, so let's plan to meet back at the bus at around eight o'clock. Then, if anyone's spotted anything of interest that the others missed, we can all traipse off to see it."

It was Lark's job to spot and point out as many species as possible for the birdwatchers, so she added, "Any of you who want to stick with me are welcome. There are also a number of great birders with us today." She pointed them out. "I'm sure any one of them would be happy to have you tag along with them.

"Just for your general information, the willow tangles are a great place to see MacGillivray's warblers and Lincoln's sparrows. You might find American dippers in the river. And, if you head west, you'll find a small pond surrounded by forests and backed by cliffs. The Cordilleran flycatcher nests along the cliffs in there, and it's the best spot to see northern water thrushes, Wilson's warblers, western tanagers and, if you're lucky, a three-toed woodpecker."

A buzz rose from the birders.

"Is the three-toed woodpecker a good bird to see?" Molly asked.

Art groaned.

"Trust me," Lark said. "It's a very good bird. Anyway, if you follow the trail, you'll come to a gate you can walk around. Keep on the path for several hundred yards until you cross the small footbridge."

The birders scattered. Lark agreed to wait while Molly used the facilities, and she scanned the trees by the compost potties looking for birds. Her eyes lit on Norberto Rincon, who had gotten off the bus and stood alone near a stand of aspen on the west side of the road. Lark sauntered over.

Norberto, dressed in black jeans and a black T-shirt, carried only a pair of beat-up binoculars. Tall and wiry, he hummed with energy and looked only slightly more relaxed today than he had at the reception when Jan had introduced him.

The loner type, thought Lark. "Hi, glad you could join us."

"Thank you." He smiled, flashing white teeth against caramel-colored skin, and dipped his dark head.

"I hear you're from Chiapas?"

"Yes." He studied her with a measured gaze.

"Do much birding there?"

96

"No."

The amusement in his eyes and his quiet scrutiny prompted her to walk away. Molly exited the toilets, and Lark called out, "Let's head toward the pond."

Norberto fell in step beside her. "I have a lot to learn."

It was the first time he'd spoken more than a word or two, and she was surprised his voice carried no accent. He spoke like he'd been educated at American schools. "I guess your job doesn't require you to have an interest in birds," she said.

"No."

"Yellow-rumped warbler, Audubon variety." Lark pointed to a tree limb high in the pine tree in front of her. She stopped, focusing her binoculars on the bird. Charcoal gray, with a bright yellow crown, throat, side patches, and rump. "Does everyone see it?"

The crowd tagging along behind her nodded. All except for Molly, who still struggled to center the bird in her binoculars. Lark had started to fall back to help, when Art moved forward. "Here, you're doing it all wrong."

"She's in good hands," Lark said, moving on. "I noticed you had no trouble spotting the warbler. You must be a hunter or sailor."

"Why do you say that?"

"Because you know how to use your binoculars too well for a nonbirder without any other spying avocation."

"You're very perceptive, Ms. Drummond."

"Lark." She moved onto the narrow path and led the way over the footbridge. "Dipper."

She spent the next few minutes pointing out birds, then settled back into her conversation. "So, you haven't worked for Jitters long."

"No."

"Don't you ever elaborate?"

"No." He grinned again. "What is it you want to know?"

Lark tipped her face, closing her eyes to the sun and basking in the warmth of the summer day. What did she want to know from him? All the things she couldn't ask Teresa, especially now that she had disappeared. "Tell me about Chiapas."

"Chiapas is the most resource-rich state in Mexico. It produces coffee, corn, and cocoa, and there's been a lot of growth in cattle ranching and timbering. It also produces a lot of hydroelectric power. But most important are the oil reserves." He dropped his head. "Yet, even with all the wealth, the poverty level is high. Very high."

The subject seemed to distress him.

"Tell me about the people."

"Most of the people in Chiapas are descended from the Mayan Indians. They speak dialects of Maya, Tzotzil, and Tzeltal. They are mostly agrarians, raising corn and coffee to support themselves. And it's a patriarchal society. First there is the household, made up of the immediate family and their plots of land, over which the elder male rules.

"Then there's the hamlet, which oversees a number of households in an area. Marriages are usually made within a hamlet, and resources are not shared."

The bitterness in his voice made Lark wonder if he'd fallen victim to the system. Maybe he'd been denied marriage to a girl he loved because of the ancient customs of his heritage. Or maybe he just felt their antiquated ways prevented them from getting ahead.

Norberto brushed a shock of dark hair off his forehead.

"Cordilleran flycatcher," Art hollered.

Lark turned to where he pointed up at the cliffs overlooking the pond.

"It's at eleven o'clock, perched high in an aspen at the base of the cliff."

She scanned, searching among the fluttering leaves for the small bird. "Good call." She turned back to Norberto, who had just dropped his binoculars to his chest. "So who oversees the hamlets?"

"They're governed by townships. That is the largest unit in Indian society, the center of culture and worship. Everyone in a township's hamlets is required to leave the household at some time and work in the township for a year. Even there, money makes a difference. The richer the farmer, the better the position he holds, the more prestige he attains, the more it benefits him spiritually.

"Townships have little communication, and each one is different. They have different customs, rules, rituals, and dress. The center of the townships is San Cristóbal de las Casas."

The city of the postmark. Lark scanned the trees for signs of birds the group had not yet spotted. "And who lives in the city?"

"Some Indians, but ladinos mostly. Mixed bloods, people who speak Spanish natively and are also agrarians, but who are more apt to be formally educated and who are more aware of the world outside of the townships. Indians trade outside very little, but ladinos manage trade. They import and export goods and oversee the trade for the townships."

Lark lowered her glasses. "That makes you a ladino, right?" She had been guessing, but Norberto's expression told her she'd guessed correctly. "So where do you buy the coffee? In the townships, or the hamlets, or do you go to the households like my partner used to do?"

"Your partner?"

"Yeah, Esther Mills, the woman who was murdered."

Norberto's eyes grew wide. "You are the owner of the Warbler Café."

"That's me. The one who knows nothing about running a coffee business."

He grabbed her, squeezing her arm in a tight grip. "Then you can help me. I'm looking for a woman. I'm looking for Teresa Cruz."

Chapter 11

Lark's blood changed to ice water in her veins. Norberto Rincon was looking for Teresa.

She thought back to Thursday night and his reaction when Buzz Aldefer had dropped a glass. Had he hidden in the shadows because he was afraid of Buzz or because he was afraid someone else might recognize him? Or had Buzz dropped the glass because he'd recognized Norberto? Either way, how did they know each other if Norberto wasn't a birdwatcher? Lark's mind sifted through the possibilities. All seemed government related.

And now Teresa was missing. Why? Had she gone into hiding underground because she recognized Norberto as a government agent, or had something happened to her?

"Let go of my arm."

"Oh, look," Molly cried out. "What's that bird?"

Lark wrenched her arm free and raised her binoculars, searching in the direction Molly pointed, forcing herself to concentrate on the job at hand. She spotted the bird low on a ponderosa pine. "It's a male three-toed woodpecker. See the yellow crown? The woodpecker was blackish, with a white strip down its back, a white line behind its eye curving downward, and its tail was black with white outer parts. Good catch, Molly."

Art glared.

At one o'clock, having avoided any further conversation with Norberto, Lark called it a day.

"Not bad for a morning," Dorothy said, an hour later, as she and Lark hurried down the deer path toward the Warbler Café. "The Endovalley group counted ninety species in under five hours. I think that might be a record."

They had changed for the memorial service at the carriage house, Lark into a pair of black slacks and white and black striped shirt, and Dorothy into a black skirt with a light pink shirt. Lark had tried getting hold of Bernie to tell him about her conversation with Norberto. The police chief wasn't in. He was probably at the Warbler for the memorial service. To be on the safe side, she'd left a message on his voice mail to call her ASAP.

Reaching the parking lot, Lark could see that the door to the Warbler stood ajar. People poured out onto the small deck, overflowing down the steps and onto the sidewalks. More people must have shown up than they'd expected. She prayed Gertie and Cecilia had been prepared.

"Never fear," Gertie said, as they entered the café through the back door. "We're ready."

The Warbler appeared transformed from yesterday when Lark had been in the offices. All traces of dust and disorder were gone. The chairs were neatly arranged, congregation-style, to face the raised seating area where a table with candles, flowers, and large posters covered with pictures of Esther had been strategically placed. A small podium and microphone stood to the right.

On the coffee bar, various types of cakes and pie had been arranged, and the smell of fresh-brewed coffee permeated the air. The wooden surface gleamed with fresh oil.

"Great job," Lark said.

"Was there ever any doubt?" Gertie flashed her a smug look, then turned to greet the first of the mourners.

Lark wandered into the back office and found Vic waiting with the minister.

"People are starting to arrive," she informed him. "Are you ready?"

As if anyone was ever ready for a funeral. The one and only she'd been to was for William Tanager, and that one she'd attended for Miriam. It was held at the Elk Park Lutheran Church. Lark had arrived early, walking in to find an empty room with an open casket. Will was laid out in his best suit and looked tan compared to the white satin casket lining.

Gertie had arrived within minutes, followed by her older sisters, Gillian and Geraldine. Geraldine and Gertie handled things well, shedding the appropriate tears into regulation hankies. But Gillian, a matron from Houston with a guilt complex that covered her travel mileage, had let out a wail and thrown herself into the casket. She'd come up covered in flesh-toned makeup, leaving William looking scarred and Miriam sputtering mad.

Lark counted her blessings this was a memorial only: no body, and no ashes.

"It's time, Vic." The minister gestured toward the office door.

Vic fingered his mustache nervously.

"You're going to get through this," Lark told him. Aside from the nervous habit, and all things considered, he looked great. His suit had been freshly pressed, his shirt collar properly starched. Instead of a cloth tie, he wore a bolo made of silver and turquoise with leather strings capped in silver. And his cowboy boots shined.

"I'm having trouble breathing."

"You're okay." She laid a hand on his sleeve and he gripped her arm.

"Stay with me?"

"Sure."

Lark walked beside him to a small love seat placed sideways behind the pulpit. From there she could see Gertie, Rachel, Dorothy, and Cecilia occupying the first row on the right. Behind them sat Harry, Eric, and the Hendersons. Paul Owens sat on the left, and he was there alone.

Why hadn't Katherine come? Did she suspect that there was more to Paul and Esther's relationship than friendship? Lark glanced sideways at Vic. Had he suspected, too? If so, he hadn't given any indications.

And there was no sign of Jan Halloway.

The service was short and simple. Several people stood and spoke, telling stories about birding with Esther. Lark didn't know what to say and so declined the opportunity. Instead, she helped cut and serve cake, pour coffee, and clear plates, until the last of the mourners headed home. She tried to catch Bernie, but he slipped away before she could stop him.

"Whew," Gertie said.

"I think our opening went well, don't you?" Cecilia asked.

"Opening?" Gertie slapped a lid on one of the coffee bins. "I'm not sure that's how I would have phrased it. More like 'our giveaway.'"

"I think it came off fine," Rachel said, scooping up a handful of glasses.

"I'm going to check the deck for glasses and stuff," Lark said. She slipped out the front door and walked to the end of the building, leaning against the railing.

"Nice out here, isn't it?" Paul Owens' voice came from behind her, causing Lark to jump. "I'm sorry," he said. "I didn't mean to scare you."

"I didn't see you out here." Lark tugged at the hem of her T-shirt. "Do you always sit around alone?"

"No." But he remained in the shadows, his face shrouded. She wished she could read his expression. Throughout the memorial service he'd maintained a stony expression, showing no emotion whatsoever. Based on the letter she'd found, he had to be hurting inside.

"I actually stuck around hoping to have a chance to talk with you for a minute."

"Oh?"

"According to Esther's attorney, you and I are business partners now."

Lark didn't mention she'd talked to Arquette as well. Instead, she played dumb. "I thought you said the Migration Alliance was the beneficiary."

"I did. I was wrong."

"When did you find that out?"

"Police Chief Crandall called me this morning and asked how I knew about the money. It seems someone had pointed out that Esther's lawyer had talked to me before I gave my speech the other night. They thought it odd I didn't know the true terms of the will. I did some checking this morning, and, apparently, I misunderstood Mr. Arquette."

Lark leaned back against the railing. Owens' motive for murder wasn't as strong if he hadn't known that he was inheriting the money. Was he smart enough to have figured that out?

"How did you know Esther, anyway?" Lark knew it was a leading question and felt guilty for asking. But not that guilty.

"We were old friends," he replied, his voice even. "I met her in Mexico a few years ago when we were both down there working." He glanced at his watch and stood. "Speaking of work, I have a dinner engagement to go to."

"Yeah? Well, have fun."

He started to walk away, then turned at the steps. "Katherine and I are hosting a small party tomorrow night up at the Black Canyon Ranch. Jan Halloway from Jitters Coffee Company will be there, along with Norberto Rincon and Buzz Aldefer. We could use a third woman. How about joining us?"

"It's awfully short notice."

"True, but we're partners now, and it might be an opportunity to get some insider information on the coffee industry."

Lark knew she ought to say no. She was helping lead the all-day volunteer's hike tomorrow, the one that Owens and the others were scheduled to attend, and there was still some planning to do. Plus, she'd been dodging Norberto.

On the other hand, they were partners. And she admired Jan Halloway. Ever since reading about her in Fortune magazine, Lark knew she wanted to grow up to be just like her: smart, attractive, and CEO of a top company before the age of forty.

"I promise, it won't be a late night," cajoled Paul. "Besides, it will give us partners a chance to get better acquainted."

Yes? No? "Sure, I'll go."

Lark agreed to meet Paul Owens and his party at the Black Canyon Ranch at five-thirty for drinks. After a cursory sweep of the porch for glasses, plates, and disposable trash, she dashed up the hill to the carriage house to change for dinner.

After a quick shower and blow dry, she braided her hair, then added a touch of mascara. Pulling on a straight black skirt and a sleeveless, Western-cut blouse with large silver buttons and a standing collar, she added a pair of black flats, two wide, silver bracelets, then studied the effect in the mirror.

Should she wear a pair of nylons, the bane of feminine society? Her legs were tan. Tan enough for dining by candlelight.

Jouncing up Black Canyon Ranch Road, she wrestled with her doubts, letting them get the best of her as she reached the top of the road.

She should have worn a nicer dress.

She should have worn her hair down.

She should have put on nylons.

What was she doing coming up here in the first place? She hardly knew these people.

She had met Paul and Katherine Saunders once before and read a few articles about Jan Halloway. That hardly classified her a member of the A team. She would turn around at the top, call the ranch, and beg off.

Lark crested the hill and made a slow loop through the parking lot, but, before she could drive away, Paul Owens hollered from the porch. "Hello the truck."

Lark slumped in her seat, then turned the truck back around and jockeyed it into a vacant spot.

"I couldn't figure out what you were doing," he said, yanking open her door. "For a minute there, I thought you were going to leave."

Lark stuffed the keys in her skirt pocket. "No way," she lied. "I was just looking for a good place to park."

"This way then." Pulling her arm through his, he escorted her up the stairs, through the foyer, and into the bar. Inside, the lights shone brightly, reflecting off the waxed hardwood floor. She definitely should have worn hose.

"I want you to meet everybody. I believe you've met my partner, Katherine. Jan Halloway."

Lark smiled and offered her hand. Katherine returned the honor, shaking hands like a dead fish. Her wrist stayed limp, her hand heavy and clammy with sweat. Jan Halloway, on the other hand, pumped back with a firm grip.

"Señor Norberto Rincon," Owens continued, "and Buzz Aldefer."

Decked out in a designer suit and Gucci loafers, Norberto nodded over his hand. Up to now, she had successfully avoided him after Molly had spotted the three-toed woodpecker. Lark was not willing to give away Teresa's whereabouts. Not that she could. Teresa had never returned to the Manor House. Lark wondered if he would try to approach her again at dinner.

Buzz stood but didn't bother to shake.

"Join us," Katherine said, patting a seat beside her. "What would you like to drink?" She signaled for the bartender, and Mike Johnson approached.

Mike owned the Black Canyon Ranch, and he and Lark went way back. They'd been what Cecilia deemed "an item" before he dumped her for his present wife, Cindy.

Lark took quiet satisfaction in the way his eyes traveled the length of her legs.

"Nice to see you," he said.

"Thanks." She crossed her legs. "I'll take a Pepsi."

"Is that all you're going to have?" Jan asked. "I thought this was a party, Paul."

A hot flush crept up Lark's face, and she fumbled for a recovery. "I'm leading the birding trip tomorrow, so…"

"Still into that?" Mike asked. It sounded more rhetorical than anything.

"Yeah."

When he had headed back to the bar, Jan twisted in her seat to face Lark. "I hear you and Paul are business partners."

Katherine's eyes narrowed.

A sore subject? Why, because of the business or because of Esther's relationship with Paul?

"That's true," Lark said, forcing her mind back to the conversation. "And it's going to be more of a challenge than I thought. I spent all of yesterday poring over the records, and some of the numbers still don't make sense."

"Oh? In what way?" Jan asked.

"Are you offering to help the competition, Jan?" drawled Buzz, "or just on the looky-loo for vulnerabilities?"

Jan's face tightened. "I was trying to be generous."

Lark decided it was time to put up her guard. "Actually, I only found one ledger where the numbers were confusing, so I brought the darn thing home. Late-night reading. I'm sure it will all fall in place soon. It's just, at the moment, I don't know anything about running a coffee company."

"For what it's worth," confided Jan, leaning forward, her blond hair falling across her face, "neither does Paul."

Had Lark been a man, the view down the front of her dress would have been cause for embarrassment. She noticed both Norberto and Paul leaned in for a closer look.

Katherine pushed back her chair. "If you'll excuse me."

Paul and Norberto stood. Buzz followed her into the foyer.

"Paul's been asking me for pointers," Jan said, never missing a beat.

"She's full of great ideas."

"That's because it's my business." Jan straightened up and tucked her hair behind her ears. "Though, I suppose, if I were smarter, I wouldn't be offering to help the competition."

Lark laughed. "You're not serious."

Jan looked taken aback.

"You can't possibly think of Chipe as competition."

Jan arched an eyebrow and shrugged her shoulder to her chin. "Our rival, then."

Lark glanced at Paul and Norberto. It was obvious Paul wasn't going to touch Jan's remark with a ten-foot pole. Norberto hadn't said a word yet.

"Chipe Coffee Company hardly vies for a share of the Jitters market," Lark said. "Jitters grossed over one billion dollars last year."

"You've been doing your homework." Jan took a sip of her vodka martini and stirred the olives around. "And you are wrong about Chipe Coffee. It's definitely competition. We bank on our reputation for being an environmentally and socially friendly company, and, from my vantage point, Chipe works to capitalize on that same market—a market Jitters Coffee Company cultivated."

Lark's Pepsi arrived, along with another round of drinks.

After a flurry of activity, Jan raised her glass in salute. "Here's to Chipe."

Lark clinked glasses with Jan, then sipped her soda. "I'll concede, we are competition, but only to a point. We do, what? One percent of the business you do? We can hardly be perceived as a serious threat."

She thought of the numbers in the ledger. Some of them were high volume. Was Esther tracking the competition? Was that what the records were about?

Jan smiled. "You're absolutely right. Jitters could squash you flatter than a tick. But, then, what's the point?" She raised her glass. "Which is why, provided you get me drunk enough over dinner, I'm going to share all my trade secrets with you."

"You won't mind if we take notes?" Paul asked.

Lark twirled the ice in her glass and waited for the laughter to abate. Jan was nothing like she had expected. The news articles depicted a young executive, maternal in her attitude toward her company and employees, yet savvy enough to grow a single storefront operation into a major, worldwide corporation. In person, she came off as a middle-aged lush with an attitude.

Lark recognized the type. They were the women of her mother's world. Women with clout, who wore their skirts short in spite of their age, craved attention, and worshiped power. Women who smiled with one side of their mouth, listened to your secrets, then used them against you at the country club. It took years to penetrate the upper circles and, once you did, you never really knew who your friends were, which kept you alone in spite of belonging.

That's what Lark had escaped by coming to Elk Park from East Haddam. Here, women brought over pie when someone died. They didn't send the hired help.

"Seriously, Lark, I'm happy to assist you in any way," Jan said. The smile. "That is, if you need help?" The fishing for secrets.

But was she fishing for information about Lark or the company? Lark steered the conversation away from Chipe Coffee and back to Jan. Two could play this game.

"Thank you. I'm just so impressed with what you've accomplished." The smile. "I know nothing. I don't know the laws of importation, testing procedures, resale packaging. But then, Jitters started out small, too, didn't they?" The jig line.

"Yes." Jan studied her momentarily, nibbling on the edge of an olive as though testing the bait. "The importing is the easy part. You follow the rules and get the coffee into the States. The important part is the resale packaging. The presentation to the buyer. Which is why Jitters is the number-one-selling specialty coffee in the U.S. today."

"Exactly how big is the Jitters Coffee Company?"

Pride filled out her voice. "At present we have approximately two thousand stores worldwide, with more opening every year. Last year, Jitters profits topped fourteen million dollars per quarter. Yet it amounts to only one-half percent of the world market share." She twirled the toothpick between her fingers, spinning the olive like a globe.

"Coffee is big business," said Norberto, speaking up for the first time. "It's a five billion dollar industry in the United States and brings in one trillion dollars' worth of gross revenue for my country every year."

Lark looked at Paul.

Wow, he mouthed.

"How much coffee is that?" Lark asked.

"Annually?" Norberto moved his hands up and down, as though weighing his words. "Give or take, Mexico exports nearly five million sixty-kilo bags a year." He let the numbers sink in, then added, "And that's only nine percent of the world market."

Jan reached over and patted his sleeve. "Norberto represents the Jitters coffee growers," she explained. "We purchase all of our Mexican coffee from Chiapas-based growers, and everything comes directly through him. It's a big responsibility. Last year alone, we purchased approximately thirty percent of our coffee from Mexico. The earnings potential is high for us because the Mexican market prices are lower than almost everywhere else."

"Why? Because of the war?" Lark realized her question sounded antagonistic, but she didn't care.

"We prefer to think of it as civil unrest."

The official version.

Paul jumped in before Lark could respond. "I want to hear what you do, young man. What exactly is your job?"

Norberto seemed startled by the question, almost as though

he didn't know the answer. He groped for words, glancing at Jan for help. "I…we…it's my job to insure the money I'm paid reaches the growers."

Paul leaned in for the kill. "Whoa. Wait a minute. If I'm understanding this right, you're saying you get paid on commission?"

Norberto looked momentarily confused, then recovered his composure and nodded his head.

"Which means, based on the number Ms. Halloway gave us, you made a hefty sum last year." Paul turned to Jan. "Why don't you purchase your coffee direct from the growers, like Esther did? It eliminates the middleman and increases your profits."

Jan's harsh laugh drew attention from as far away as the bar. "You have to consider how much coffee Esther purchased. Maybe five hundred bags a year, at the most. Jitters purchased just under one hundred thousand bags last year. We're feeding a worldwide market with a humongous appetite."

Lark's annoyance meter exploded. "Are you putting down Esther's attempts to preserve bird habitat?"

"No, you're misreading what I said."

Lark knew she should hold her tongue, but, what the heck, she was on a roll. "Esther traveled to Mexico and paid the growers directly because she believed they were being ripped off by the large corporations and the middlemen." She warmed to her subject, and her voice grew louder. "She insured that she purchased only shade-grown, bird-supportive coffee. And, in order to make a difference, paid out more per kilo for the product, direct to the grower."

Jan brushed Lark's comment aside with the flick of her hand. "The coffee industry is not a cause, Lark. It's business. If you remember to think in a businesslike manner, you'll survive." The subtext: If you don't, you'll die, and I'll dance on your grave. "I'm sure you'll do fine." The smile. "And, now you have me curious. Exactly how much did Esther pay per kilo?" Fishing.

Lark moved away from the bait. "I'm not sure. I'd have to look at the records."

"Ballpark figure."

"Esther claimed she paid seventy percent over market," Paul said. "What would that amount to?"

"I'm not drunk enough to tell you that yet." Jan sipped her martini. "Not that it matters. What matters is, it's not the growers who need the money, it's the workers. It's the growers who pay the field hands poverty wages."

"Do you even know what the average coffee picker makes per day?" asked Norberto.

"No," admitted Lark, forcing herself to cool down.

"Three dollars a day."

"That may be true, but most of the farm workers are family members who benefit from the mere existence of the crop. Even the larger farms are family-run operations." Lark was glad she remembered parts of Esther's spiel. "Jitters pays you less per bag than Esther pays her growers. Then you take a percentage off the top. Tell me how you think that's fair."

Norberto's expression changed. Where sorrow had been written just moments before, anger now reigned. His eyes glittered with the self-righteousness of someone falsely accused.

"I'll tell you what," Jan said. "You tell me what Esther pays her growers per kilo, and I'll tell you what percentage of that lines the grower's pockets."

"Better his than the middleman's," countered Lark, unable to resist getting in one last dig. The comment crossed the proverbial line, and she clamped her mouth shut.

Norberto's face flushed. Jan glared. Lark met the stare, refusing to break eye contact. The air crackled between them. Finally, Jan looked away.

Lark tugged at the hem of her skirt and tried changing her tone. "Look, all I'm saying is that the organic grower is a small businessman. Just like me. He needs the profits in order to sustain his business. Without the extra money, he can't continue to grow coffee in a shade tree environment. He'll be forced to convert his land, destroying shade environment and valuable bird habitat."

Jan took a swig of her martini and banged the glass down on the cocktail table. "Listen, bird girl, there is no possible way

Jitters can insist that its suppliers pay more than they already are to the farmers. We pay fair market value for our products. We do everything possible to help combat the poverty and sustain the environment. I'll have you know, last year we contributed over one million dollars to social and environmental programs around the world. Why? Because that's the type of company we are."

Which was what percentage? Multiplying the quarterly profits by four, and factoring in the one million dollars in contributions, Lark quickly calculated that Jitters annually donated around one and a half percent of their profits. Without knowing the exact numbers, she couldn't factor what Chipe's percentage would be. She could only hope it was higher.

Chapter 12

"Our table's ready," announced Katherine. "I've left Buzz to arrange the seating."

Jan pulled her hand from Norberto's sleeve. "Saved by the dinner bell."

Lark forced a smile and stood, smoothing the wrinkles from the front of her skirt. The gesture brushed away some of her anger. Business was business, and Jan's job was to make money for Jitters. Jan was limited in how much she could do, just like Lark was. For the second time that night, her thoughts ran to Teresa.

Katherine led the way to the dining room. Paul brought up the rear. Old guard, old manners, old money, at least in Katherine's case. They followed customs culled over generations by the upper classes, emulated by the middle classes, and often disdained or disregarded by the lower classes. Customs that dictated who went first, who came last. Lark fell in behind Jan.

"Lark, you sit here by me," Buzz said, pulling out a chair.

Her seat touched the chair, and instantly a waiter appeared to spread a napkin across her lap. A busboy stepped forward and filled her glass with water.

A pair of pale yellow candles burned in silver candlesticks at either end of the table. Translucent china in delicate patterns of a similar color adorned the iris-blue tablecloth. Crystal glasses sparkled in the candlelight.

Katherine sat down at one end of the table, Paul at the other. Jan and Norberto sat across from Buzz and Lark. Boy, girl, boy, girl.

"Isn't this lovely?" Katherine said. "I hope you don't mind, but I took the liberty of ordering appetizers while I was checking on our table."

On cue, a silver tray of crackers and pâté arrived. Lark took some, then passed them to Buzz. If Katherine had been ordering hors d'oeuvres, where had he been?

Lark busied herself with a butter knife. "Major," she said,

hoping to turn the conversation in a new direction. "Tell me again, what is your connection to the Migration Alliance?"

"I'm just here to keep the United States Air Force apprised of what's happening with our fine feathered friends." Buzz popped a cracker into his mouth and reached for another. "Most of my time is spent in Houston, reading reports."

For a desk jockey he looked remarkably fit. Tall and graying, broad shoulders stretched the seams of his dinner jacket. Strong cords bulged in his neck, threatening to pop the collar button off his white shirt.

"Now, don't be modest," said Owens. "Buzz spends a lot of his time in Mexico, volunteering at the Hawkwatch site, helping Pronatura out with tours, that sort of thing."

"So the government pays you to birdwatch?" Lark pretended not to notice him choke on his food. "Sign me up." She noticed that Norberto watched him intently.

Buzz wiped his mouth on his napkin. "Excuse me, but I can't say anyone's ever asked me that question before."

"You don't have to answer," Katherine told him. She turned to Lark. "Suffice it to say, he works with our national security in mind."

Was Katherine protecting him? "Forgive me," Lark said. "I didn't mean it like—"

"No, no. Not to worry," interrupted Buzz, brushing a hand across his flattop. "The Air Force's interest is in the migratory patterns of birds. We need to learn more about their migration in order to understand how their flights might impact military maneuvers. And how our operations impact their flights." He slathered pâté on a cracker. "I've only been observing in Mexico for the past several years. I'm still learning. But I can tell you one thing: Be careful flying a plane in or out of Chiapas in March, or you might eat a hawk for lunch."

"I'll heed the advice."

"Are you satisfied?" Katherine asked coldly.

Lark toyed with the drips of condensation forming on her crystal water glass. "I just have one more question."

"You don't know when to stop, do you?" snapped Jan.

Katherine glared at all of them. Norberto hid a smile behind his napkin. Paul craned his neck and tugged at his shirt collar.

"Have any of you ever seen a red-faced warbler?"

The rest of dinner passed with talk of birds and adventures, then about nine o'clock, Lark excused herself.

"No, don't go, yet," Paul protested. "We're just about to order after-dinner drinks."

"I really have to go. I'm leading the hike to Paris Pond in the morning, and we start out at five o'clock."

After another polite volley of protest, Owens decided to leave, too, and walked her out to the truck. The moon rode high in the sky, bathing the parking lot in shades of dawn and dusk. Trees stood like sentinels of the forest, dark against the whitewashed ground.

Boop.

"Did you hear that?" Lark turned toward the pine trees that lined the road leading out of the parking lot. She cocked her head. "Listen."

Another hollow boop came from high in the trees.

"Your call," Paul said.

"A flammulated owl."

Paul nodded.

Lark squinted, trying to spot the bird among the trees. "Do you see it?" she asked.

Paul moved right, then pointed. "There, on the branch. In this moonlight, you can even see its dark eyes and mottled plumage."

"What are you two looking at?" Jan asked, stumbling down the porch steps. "Oops."

"Careful there, Jan." Buzz scooped her up before she hit the ground, setting her on her feet. "Whew, boy. Which one of us is driving?"

Lark raised a finger to her lips.

"Ohhh," Buzz opened his eyes wide, then, contorting his face, mimicked Lark. "Shhhh, everybody." He looked around, swiveling his head from side to side, then let out a deep, booming laugh. "Why are we being so quiet?"

"Because there's an owl in the trees," whispered Lark. She

pointed, but the creature was gone.

Buzz craned his neck. "I don't see him."

That's because you frightened him away.

Jan let out a peal of laughter. "Did someone say we're going hiking tomorrow? I'm going to need an Advil. Better yet, a bottle of Advil."

Lark climbed into her truck.

She waited for Owens to wheel out of the parking lot ahead of her. Following at a slow pace, she maintained a safe distance, content to bring up the rear. His car lurched in the potholes, weaving from side to side. Lark could see Jan, wedged in the backseat between Norberto and Buzz, her head lolling back and forth.

What were Paul and Katherine thinking, bringing those three to Migration Alliance? It was clear none of them gave a hoot about birds. To Jan and Norberto, shade-grown, organic coffee spelled money. Plain and simple, everything perched on the bottom line. The increased consciousness among Americans might force them to tout the environmental message, but the facts remained: Profit ruled the day.

But what was Buzz's interest? It wasn't money. There was no financial gain for him. And it wasn't the birds. Drunk or sober, a serious birder would have shown more interest in a flammulated owl. So, what was he watching? The people? She'd read stories about spies who used bird-watching as a cover. Maybe Major Buzz Aldefer was in Mexico ferreting out intel?

Ahead of her, Owens flipped on his blinker and turned left onto Raptor House Road. Lark stopped her truck at the junction and watched him drive away. Several things about the past couple of days had been bothering her: the odd numbers in Esther's ledger, the letter written by Paul, and tonight's conversation about business.

Lights shone from the windows at Bird Haven. Rachel was still up. Time to pay her a visit.

Rachel came to the door in her pj's, red hair tumbling around her shoulders. "Lark, what are you doing here?" Rachel peered past her into the moonlit night.

"Got a minute?"

"Is everything all right?" She stepped aside to let Lark enter, eyeing her outfit.

"Peachy, except I just came from the weirdest dinner party." Lark brushed past her, and Rachel closed and locked the door.

"What do you mean?" She gestured for Lark to follow and padded ahead of her down the hall toward the family room. Irish folk music, piped through a central stereo system, played softly in the background.

Lark plopped down in the easy chair and briefed Rachel on the highlights: who was there, the conversation, the nuances. "Things just seemed out of kilter. Like Jan. She kept trying to find out how much Esther paid per kilo for the coffee she purchased."

"She's in that business." Rachel shrugged. "Did you tell her?"

"No, but Paul divulged the fact that Esther paid seventy percent above market price. If Jan can add and multiply, she can figure it out." Lark kicked her shoes off and wiggled her toes in the plush carpeting. "What I want to know is why it mattered to her so much."

"Chipe Coffee is her competition. It's good business to know."

"Maybe, though I'd hardly classify Chipe as her toughest competitor." Lark studied the rug. "Maybe she thinks Norberto is ripping her off."

"You're smart enough to do the math in reverse. What's he getting paid per kilo?"

"Nobody would say. Paul even Jan asked point blank, and she replied that she wasn't drunk enough to give away trade secrets."

Rachel repositioned a cushion behind her back. "So she wouldn't give you any information, but she kept asking how much Esther paid for coffee."

"That's about the size of it. The only stats she offered were on the number of sixty-kilo bags Jitters purchased every year and the number of dollars they donated for social and bird habitat-related programs." Lark toyed with the hem of her skirt.

"It got me to thinking. Did I tell you about Esther's ledger?"

"No."

Lark described the book. "I have no idea what the numbers mean. She wrote dates in there, too, so I think she was keeping track of someone else's shipments."

Rachel pulled her hair back and looped it into a knot. "It's easy enough to find out the market price of coffee using the Internet." She uncurled herself off the sofa. "Want to try?"

"I'm game."

Lark followed Rachel back to the bedroom suite situated in a wing off the front hallway. It consisted of a bedroom, an up-to-the-minute bathroom, and a small office. Rachel commandeered the desk chair and booted up the computer, swirling the mouse on the mouse pad. "Let's try searching 'Mexican Coffee.'"

The computer whirred, and the search engine located a cookie recipe, several sites for a New Mexican gift packaging firm, and twenty-five companies selling roasted organic coffee from Chiapas but featuring no additional information on the country or its political troubles.

"Jitters is listed here. Let's check it out." Rachel clicked on the connect bar, and the Jitters site popped onto the screen. A coffee plant dominated the screen, with bean buttons labeled to lead you through the pages. The home page carried information on the company, with links to worldwide store locations, franchise information, and purchasing information on bulk coffee and merchandise. The pricing was competitive, but there was still no specific information on the coffee coming out of Chiapas, Mexico.

"Try 'organic coffee,'" suggested Lark, pulling up a straight-backed chair. The results were similar: recipes and companies, like Jitters and Chipe, selling beans.

Inputting "Mexico+coffee," they discovered a site with information on the struggle between the Zapatistas and the government over coffee production, but nothing about coffee exportation.

Finally, after half an hour of trial and error, they stumbled upon the site of the Mexican Coffee Council. Rachel downloaded the information, and Lark pored over the printouts.

"It says here, Mexico exports approximately four point five million sixty-kilo bags of coffee a year. Of that, only about sixty thousand bags are classified organic. Chiapas is the largest producer."

"I have a question," Rachel said. "Can coffee that's not organic be considered shade-grown?"

"Not by my definition."

"I'm serious, Lark."

Lark lowered the pages, and stared at Rachel, who was still hunched over the computer. "Technically, I suppose so. There are some shade-grown farmers that still use pesticides to help control insect damage."

"Okay, here we go," Rachel said, scrolling down the screen. "It says here that coffee prices range from eighty-five cents per pound to one dollar twenty-four cents per pound."

Lark doodled the numbers on the back of the printouts. "Did you know that most people pay more for a cappuccino than the average Mexican coffee picker makes in a day?"

"No."

The matter-of-factness in Rachel's reply, the acceptance, fit with the relative opulence of their surroundings. They lived in luxury, while out there people struggled to survive.

Rachel reached for the mouse and logged off, shattering the profundity of the moment. "Want some ice cream? I need a bedtime snack."

Lark dogged her heels down the hallway. "What if Norberto was ripping Jan off, and Esther figured it out? What if she threatened to tell Jan?"

"Then that might be a reason to murder her," Rachel said, pulling a carton of ice cream out of the freezer. She scooped heaping mounds of chocolate into two clear glass bowls. "Provided, of course, we're talking about a lot of money?"

"I'm guessing, but say Norberto sells thirty thousand bags of coffee to Jitters a year..." Lark calculated the math in her head. "If you take sixty kilos times two point two..." She chewed her lip. "That gives you one hundred thirty-two pounds. Times that by around a dollar ten per pound, and...He's pulling in gross around one hundred forty-five dollars a bag. That amounts to—

"

"Try this." Rachel tossed her the calculator from beside the phone.

Lark ran the numbers again. "If the numbers are right, after paying off the farmers, Norberto would be banking around four hundred thousand dollars a year."

"That's a lot of money. But, maybe he's not the one profiting."

Lark sucked on a bite of chocolate ice cream. "Then who?"

"What about Jan Halloway?"

Lark rolled the idea in her mind. "I don't think she'd take those kinds of risks, not with her business. Jitters Coffee Company means everything to her. Besides, she already makes great money."

"Hmumm." Rachel clinked her spoon in her bowl. "Do they still consider Vic a suspect?"

"As far as I know. And maybe with reason." Lark told Rachel about finding the love letter from Paul.

"Do you still have it?"

Lark remembered stuffing it in the pocket of her shorts. What had she done with it after that? Teresa had been waiting for her when she arrived home, and Velof. She'd changed for the MA opening ceremonies and tossed the shorts in the laundry. The letter must still be there. "I left it at home."

"You need to show it to Bernie," Rachel said. She cleared the dishes from the counter and wiped it with a wet rag. "And you need to tell him about tonight and this afternoon."

Lark found her shoes and slipped them on. "You know, there's another person worth considering as a suspect."

"Wait, who do we have so far?"

"Vic, the mistreated common law husband. Paul Owens. Katherine Saunders, the possessive partner. Teresa, Norberto, and Jan."

"Who's left?"

"Buzz Aldefer, the guy assigned to MA from the Air Force. He claims he's interested in migration patterns of birds, and Paul told me he volunteers at Hawkwatch in Mexico, but I think he might be a spy."

"A what?"

"You know, a spy. James Bond, double oh seven." Lark twirled her truck keys on her finger. "Don't look so shocked. Birdwatching is a great cover. It would be a perfect way for a military man to get intel on what's happening with Mexico's civil uprising. He puts on his birding vest, treks into the backcountry, and no one's the wiser." Lark flipped her braid off her shoulder, feeling it slide down her back. She liked that theory. "I'll bet the Air Force talked Katherine into supplying the cover, and that's why she was so protective of him when I asked what he did in Mexico. And I'll bet that's why Norberto reacted so violently when Buzz broke a glass on the patio Thursday night. He probably recognized him. Heck, maybe Norberto's passing him secrets about the people in Chiapas."

"I think you need to go home and go to bed." Rachel walked Lark toward the door. "Though, that type of theory would be easy enough for you to check out."

Lark bristled. "I'm not calling my father."

Rachel leaned against the edge of the front door, rocking it back and forth. "It was just a thought."

"A bad one. I'm not doing it." Lark had already called her dad, the senator, once this summer to ask for his help. She had no intention of making a habit of it. "The object is to prove to Daddy that I'm self-sufficient, not prove to him I'm needy."

It was nearly one o'clock in the morning by the time Lark parked her truck in front of the carriage house. The Drummond lounge still hopped. Several partygoers were guzzling last call on the patio. Their laughter floated through the pines like the hoots of an owl, and Lark prayed they would keep it down to a dull roar. She had to be up early.

A harsh laugh sliced the air. She recognized it as Jan Halloway's. Lark heard her telling someone how the nightlife in San Francisco would just be warming up now, and Lark closed the door of the truck with a soft click. Last thing she wanted was to be heard.

Scooting along the sidewalk, she hugged the side of the carriage house. The moonlight cast eerie shadows, calling out the ghosts that haunted the upper floors of the Drummond Hotel. On nights like this one, guests complained of hearing a woman weeping and light footsteps pacing the upper halls. The Lady of the Drummond.

Lark glanced up at the top floor. A shadow crossed a window. A curtain fluttered.

With the hairs on her arms standing on end, Lark bounded up the front steps. She flung open the door and stepped into the living room, her foot striking something hard. Her ankle twisted, and she fell, landing hard on the wooden floor.

Her elbow smacked the door frame.

The screen banged shut against her head.

Damn. Lark pushed herself up, her fingers landing on a thick book. What's this doing here?

Struggling to her feet, she tripped over several more books on the floor, then waited for her eyes to adjust to the dark. Dappled moonlight illuminated the living room. Books lay strewn everywhere on the floor.

"What the…?" She reached for the light switch.

A dark figure struck her from behind, knocking her to the floor. Sprawling on her face, she slid. The couch loomed in front of her. Her head cracked against the wooden leg.

Scrambling to her feet, she stumbled backward toward the door.

She was struck again, this time from the side, and her legs buckled beneath her. Her leg twisted as she fell, and the torque on her ankle was so strong she thought the bones would snap. Allowing her body to roll, she released the pressure and clambered to her feet.

Where was he? Where the hell was he?

She spotted a flash of movement out of the corner of her eye. A large book crashed toward her head, and she raised her arms, deflecting the blow. Anger and fear combined, and in one movement, the victim became the aggressor.

"Who are you?" she demanded. Her hand groped for a weapon, something to defend herself with, and struck the telephone. The phone system was hooked into the Drummond's. Knocking away the receiver, she punched 0. A high-pitched beep punctuated the darkness and froze the moment in time.

"Good evening, Drummond Hotel." Velof's voice sounded faint and far away.

"Stephen, this is Lark!" she screamed.

Her attacker bolted. Man or woman, tall or short, in the blur of motion, Lark couldn't tell. Dressed in black, hands gloved, face covered by a ski mask, the intruder fled toward the kitchen.

"Lark! Where have you—"

"Stephen, there is someone in my house. Call security."

At the kitchen door, her attacker turned. Lark pressed her hand to her forehead and felt a warm, sticky sensation. Moonlight shone on her assailant. Boldly written on the forehead of the mask were the letters EZLN. Esther's killer had come to call.

Chapter 13

A half hour later, Lark stood beside Bernie Crandall, an ice bag pressed to her head, eyeing the chaos. Books, their spines cracked and broken, littered the floors. Drawers stood open, their contents scattered. Several dishes were broken. And the pantry'd been rifled and cereal boxes emptied onto the floor.

"Okay, so you're sure this guy was wearing the same mask."

"Positive."

"Then the question is, what the hell does Esther's killer want with you?"

"I did witness the murder."

"Yeah, Drummond, but you didn't see anything. Nope," Crandall said, picking up a shard of pottery. "It looks to me like he was lookin' for somethin'. Too bad about your plates."

Dismayed by the mess and furious that someone dared to invade her personal space and destroy her personal things, Lark fought back tears.

"You got any ideas what he was after?"

Lark moved her head. Pain sliced across the back of her eyes. "No. It didn't look like he was carrying anything, either."

"Did you stumble across anything recently that someone might have wanted? Something small enough to stick in a pocket or down the back of your pants?"

"No."

"Did your new partner give you anything?"

"No—" Lark stopped as it occurred to her. The ledger. "I brought home a business ledger." Why hadn't she thought of that up until now? She must have been hit harder than she thought. "It—"

Officer Klipp, gun slapping against uniformed thigh, clanked in and interrupted. "Whoever was here has cleared out, Chief. He must have found what he wanted. The only two rooms trashed are the kitchen and living room."

"Where was this ledger you mentioned?" Crandall asked.

"On the bookshelf." She pointed to the carnage on the floor.

"Okay, have the boys dust for fingerprints. We're going to

want to search this room carefully." Crandall set down the fragment of stoneware and dusted his hands together. "How about you and I have a talk in your office?"

"Shouldn't we look for the ledger?"

"When the boys are through. If we searched for it now, we'd be compromising evidence. Let's go."

Lark obeyed, leading Crandall through the back door of the Drummond whereby avoiding the guests out front, who'd been rousted by the lights and sirens of Elk Park's finest. Jan Halloway had been in the crowd, still wearing her dinner outfit. And Norberto, dressed in black jeans and a T-shirt.

The intruder had been dressed in black.

Paul and Katherine had been there, too, outside in pajamas and robes. She didn't remember seeing Buzz Aldefer.

Stopping in the hotel kitchen, Lark loaded a tray with coffee mugs, a carafe of hot coffee, and a handful of creamers. "Do you take sugar?"

"Nope."

When they rounded the corner from the dining room, Velof jumped up from the desk.

"We're eluding the mob," explained Crandall. "Why don't you join us?"

"This way," Lark said.

Velof opened the office door, and Crandall walked in, taking Lark's chair behind the desk. Lark grabbed a visitor's chair opposite. Velof closed the door and stood gazing out the window.

"Okay, so who wants to tell me what happened tonight?"

"I'll start," volunteered Velof. "There's not much to tell. Peter Jacobs called in sick, so I was forced to cover his shift." Velof looked pointedly in Lark's direction. She ignored him. Managing a staff was like being a mother. As much as possible, you ignored the squabbles.

"I sent over chicken soup," he continued, "but Jacobs wasn't there, so—"

"Just tell me what happened later."

"I worked," snapped Velof, "until Lark called for security." He paused. "For what it's worth, I believe Jacobs left with the

125

Mexican girl, which means we'll need to run an ad for evening help."

Lark repositioned her ice bag. "You think he left?"

"Yes. His suitcase is gone, and some of his clothes."

Crandall toyed with the stapler on Lark's desk. "How do you know that?"

"I searched his room."

"You what?" Lark pulled herself forward in her chair. "Stephen, you're not allowed to use your key to enter another employee's private space."

He stiffened. "I was suspicious, and rightly so."

"That may be, but—" She heard her tone. The mother scolding. Children!

"How about Lark's space?" Crandall asked. "Have you ever been there uninvited?"

Both Lark and Velof swiveled to face him. Lark waited for the answer.

"No." Velof sounded shocked at the suggestion.

"And what did you do after Lark called?"

"I forwarded the phones to voice messaging and walked over to the carriage house. I couldn't see any reason to call out security if the culprit had already fled. I assumed it was a child's prank. I must say, it wasn't until after I noticed everything flung about the living room that I knew it was serious. She's normally quite neat."

"How would you know?" Lark asked, convinced now that he had been spying on her.

Velof reddened.

"You're fired," she said.

"I am the best help you've got!"

"Maybe so, but poking your nose around my house or anyone's private rooms is despicable. In fact, it's illegal, isn't it, Bernie?"

"Yep." Crandall poured himself a mug of coffee. "Getting back to the break-in, did you see anything suspicious before Lark called? Anyone hanging around the lobby who shouldn't have been there?"

"Wait, I'm not quite finished—" Lark wasn't quite ready to

drop the illegal-to-spy-on-your-employer business.

"No," interrupted Velof. "I checked periodically to see if there were any lights on over there, or if her truck was parked out front. I wanted to talk to her. But I saw nothing suspicious at all."

"Thank you, Steve. I'll let you know if I need anything else."

"Stephen," muttered Velof.

"Whatever." Crandall stood up and steered him toward the door.

Velof looked at Lark. "Should I mind the desk or get my things and leave?"

Lark glared, pushing back in her seat and letting the ice bag rest in her lap. She needed him at the desk.

"Well?"

"I'm thinking." Velof was all she had with Jacobs missing in action. "Okay, mind the desk."

"So I'm not fired?"

"Not yet. But we're not through discussing this."

"You need to chill out, Drummond," Crandall said, shutting the door behind Velof. "Good help's hard to find."

"Tell me about it."

"So what happened?"

"You heard it before. I got back around one o'clock, walked through the door, and was attacked. I managed to dial the phone, and Velof called security."

Crandall rested his elbows on the desk and his chin in his hand. "I'm looking for details, not the big picture."

"Details. For starters, the guy was wearing a black ski mask with the initials EZLN."

"Do you know anyone besides Teresa who might have a connection to a hat like that?"

"Norberto. He works out of Chiapas and buys coffee in the area. But, honestly, any one of the people I was with at dinner tonight would have had access to such a mask. They've all traveled to the area on business or pleasure."

"Pleasure?"

"It's a great birdwatching spot."

"So tell me about this dinner party. For starters, who was

there?"

"Paul Owens, Katherine Saunders, Jan Halloway, Buzz Aldefer, Norberto Rincon, and me."

"And did anyone else know you were going to dinner?"

"I might have mentioned it at the Warbler while we were cleaning up after the memorial service for Esther."

"So Vic might have overheard?"

"Yeah. On the flip side, Teresa wasn't there."

Crandall seemed to chew on the information. "Okay, so go back to the beginning. Did you notice anything when you pulled in the parking lot?"

Lark thought back. "I climbed out of the truck. I heard Jan Halloway was on the patio, so I stayed in the shadows, trying to get into the house without having to talk to her."

"Now, who's Halloway again?"

"She's the CEO of Jitters Coffee Company."

"Right." He made a note for himself. "And why were you avoiding her?"

"Because she was drunk. I just didn't feel like dealing with her anymore tonight."

"Okay, go on."

"Where was I?"

"Cut the crap, Drummond. You were sneaking up your front walk, and…"

"I saw someone peeking out one of the top-floor windows. After that I—"

"Do you know which one?" Crandall asked. "Is there a way to find out whose room it is?"

"Sure. It was the second from the right, top floor, room four twenty, the Lady of Drummond's room." She came around the desk and flipped on the computer. "We have everything on a program now. I just call up the number and…voilà." She pointed to the screen. "The room's assigned to Buzz Aldefer."

Buzz was the only one at dinner unaccounted for on the patio tonight.

Crandall rubbed his jaw. "You mentioned a ledger. What's that all about?"

"I brought it home from the Warbler. It's an inventory and

supply ledger, but it had some weird dates and numbers recorded in it, numbers I can't decipher. I figured that maybe if I brought it home and took my time over it, I could figure out what they mean."

"Any ideas?"

"I think maybe—and it's a big maybe—Esther was tracking the coffee shipments of her competitors. She made all sorts of notations in the margins: names of people, descriptions of things. I didn't get a really good chance to look at it."

Crandall rolled Lark's chair back from the desk. "Let's go see if we can find it."

Lark left the dirty mugs and empty carafe for Velof to clear. In the Drummond kitchen, she stopped long enough to refill the ice bag. The stainless steel counters, the subzero refrigerators, and oversized sinks gleamed in the fluorescent lighting casting eerie blue shadows on whitewashed walls.

"Who would have known about the ledger?" Crandall asked, his deep voice echoing.

"Everyone at dinner tonight."

"Paul Owens?"

"Sure," Lark said. "He was there when I admitted I was having trouble understanding some of the information."

"Give me everyone's names again. I may want to talk with them."

"Owens, Katherine Saunders, Jan Halloway, Norberto Rincon, and Buzz Aldefer." The shadow at the window.

"Did Teresa know about the book?"

Lark tried to think. She knew she hadn't said anything to her about it. "I don't know. She may have seen me with it. She was waiting for me on the porch when I brought it home."

When they reached the carriage house, Crandall sent one of his men down to check on the Warbler; then he Rachel asked to describe the ledger.

"It was plain brown, leather. Paper-sized. I stuck it on the kitchen bookshelf."

Crandall, Lark, and two officers searched. After about fifteen minutes, head pounding, Lark sat back on her heels.

"It's not here," she declared. "The ledger's missing."

At five a.m. the next morning, Lark woke up to Shania Twain belting "Feel Like a Woman." She'd considered canceling out on the hike after last night's break-in, then changed her mind when she'd realized all of the others would be there. By breaking into her house, the killer had made this personal. She refused to wimp out.

Groaning, she tumbled out of bed, gulped down three painkillers, and crawled into the shower, turning the spray to sting. Between Bernie insisting she answer more questions and Velof demanding to know if he still had a job, she'd ended up with less than two hours of sleep. Barely enough to function on, even without a head wound. Then again, Thomas Edison claimed a human being performed best when they slept only twenty minutes out of every four hours, and he was a genius. Maybe sleep deprivation helped one to see things more clearly.

Climbing out of the shower, Lark toweled off, pulling on a pair of jeans and a long-sleeved T-shirt. The hike today took them up the east face of Elk Mountain to Paris Pond. Not quite as strenuous as the hike up Long's Peak, but they would still reach twelve thousand feet by the time they reached the pond and turnaround point. No place to be in shorts, even on a sunny day.

Lark grabbed her jacket and binoculars and surveyed the mess in the kitchen. She and Crandall had picked up a lot of the books looking for the ledger, but many still lay open on the floor, spines cracked and broken. Paper clips made the going treacherous, along with pencils and pens, sticky note pads, scissors, pliers, rubber bands, and the occasional phone drawer treasures still scattered across the linoleum.

She snatched up her boots at the back door and pulled them on, then shrugged into her jacket out front on the stoop. The air felt nippy, a welcome relief from the eighty-degree temperatures. Maybe there was a cold front moving in.

When she arrived at the bus, Dorothy was there to greet her. "You look horrible, Lark. You weren't out drinking all night with Jan, were you?" She gestured toward the Jitters CEO, who looked pale and haggard as she sat on a nearby picnic bench.

"No." Lark told Dorothy about the break-in and the missing ledger. "Heavens. Are you okay?"

"I'm here."

"What's wrong, Dorothy?" Cecilia asked, scurrying over.

Lark repeated a simplified version of the story. "Pass it on."

"Oh my. Maybe you shouldn't be going on the hike today, dear."

"I'm fine. A little bump on the head, that's all. I wouldn't miss it." Out of the corner of her eye, she could see Norberto talking with Jan. Excusing herself, she edged away from the sisters and closer to the couple, until she could overhear their conversation.

"Tell me why I'm doing this," moaned Jan, clutching a cup of coffee, her eyes red-rimmed and bloodshot.

"Because it is part of the convention, and you're the guest of honor," replied Norberto. "It's your job."

At the word job, Jan perked up and tried pasting on a happier face.

The day-long hike was traditionally called the Volunteer's Hike. Every year, those who donated their time and energy to making the Migration Alliance convention a success were treated with a one-on-one birding experience with the MA guests of honor. Today's guests consisted of Jan, Norberto, and Buzz, along with Paul, Katherine, and half a dozen other special presenters, all knowledgeable birders, most gung-ho.

The volunteers included Dorothy, Cecilia, and Gertie, along with fifteen or twenty other generous souls from all across the country. Lark was the designated group leader.

Once everyone had assembled, Lark climbed up on the short retaining wall and waited for the buzz of conversation to die down. "Can everyone hear me okay?"

"Speak up," shouted someone in back.

"I don't know why I'm your appointed leader," she said more loudly, rewarded by a thumbs-up signal from the back and a pulsing in her head. "I'm sure it's only because I know the area, There are certainly better-qualified birders with us today." Balanced somewhat precariously on the rough wall, Lark repositioned her feet and pulled out a park map. "We're hiking up to Paris Pond today. We'll go by bus to the trailhead, hike about four miles in, and climb about two thousand feet in elevation. Everyone needs a sweater and water bottle. And some of you may decide to stop at Alpine Meadow, just before we cross Alpine Creek and start our ascent to Paris Pond."

A woman near the back raised her hand.

"Yes, Harriet?" Lark asked.

"Is the walk fairly easy most of the way?"

"It's gentle to Alpine Creek. That's about two and a half miles in. After that, the climb is steeper, and there are a few places where the path narrows enough that if you have any fear of heights, you'll be uncomfortable." Lark scanned the crowd. "Anyone is free to stop and turn around whenever they'd like. The reason we're ascending to Paris Pond is to give you a chance to spot white ptarmigan and brown-capped rosy-finches."

"What other species will we see?" shouted a man Lark didn't recognize.

"We'll have a fair chance of seeing blue grouse, three-toed woodpeckers, and pine grosbeak, along with the red-naped and Williamson's sapsuckers. There's potential for black swifts, and a good chance of seeing the Rocky Mountain subspecies of fox sparrow." She glanced at her watch. "Okay, we'll be leaving in ten minutes. Anyone who needs to, grab a jacket, get water, and use the bathroom."

Lark climbed down off the wall, careful not to jar anything. Her head hurt the worst, but her right ankle was tender from being twisted when she tripped over the book. No sense in exacerbating either by being too active.

Gertie stopped her en route to the bathroom. "I overheard one of the hotel guests saying you had a break-in at your house last night. Is that true?"

"Yeah." Lark told her about the intruder and the missing ledger.

"What's Crandall doing about it?"

"Investigating. He said he might question a few people, but he didn't act like it was a big rush."

"That figures." Gertie worried her bottom lip with her teeth, then asked, "Rachel is supervising at the Warbler today, isn't she?"

"That was the plan. She and all three of the kids."

"Don't you think one of us should call her, just to make sure she's up?"

"Trust me, Gertie, if she can run a million dollar advertising campaign, she can handle the coffee shop for a day."

Gertie flipped her head, making her bob bob. "You know, running the Warbler's not as easy as it looks."

Before Lark could answer, Dorothy came charging up the sidewalk. She wore blue jeans, hiking boots, and a bright pink jacket zipped up to her throat. She'd crushed a pink baseball cap over her curls. "Here," she said, thrusting a walkie-talkie into Lark's hand. "I have one, too. Consider it a safety precaution. Walk away from me, and we'll test them out."

Gladly. Anything to escape Gertie. Lark went in search of Velof.

The walkie-talkie cracked to life. "Testing, testing," squawked Dorothy. "Do you read me? Over."

"Loud and clear," replied Lark, squelching the volume. Talk about scaring the birds.

"What is that contraption?" Velof asked. He looked saggy this morning himself. Dark circles rimmed his eyes, and one piece of his hair stuck up unbridled.

"They're Dorothy's idea," Lark said, brandishing the walkie-talkie. "Go home, Stephen. Get some rest."

"Jacobs still hasn't shown up. Neither has Teresa. I'll bet those are your culprits. Are you sure no money was missing?"

"Why would they break into my house for money? Jacobs had a key to the cash registers."

"Good point."

Besides, Lark liked Teresa. She didn't relish the thought that she'd stolen the ledger, then run off with Jacobs. "Maybe Teresa's just hiding out and took Jacobs with her. He did seem to have a crush on her."

"When piglets fly."

"That would be one for the life lists." Lark smiled. "Look, Velof, go home and get some rest. The reservations clerks can

133

hold down the fort while you grab forty winks. I'll be back around four this afternoon."

Stephen smoothed down his hair. "An owner presence is required to make a business run its best."

"Tomorrow's Monday. I'll be around all day. I promise."

The bus ride up to the trailhead was uneventful. Lark's head ceased pounding, and Jan caught a short nap. Several diehards called out birds spotted through the bus windows along the roadside: a red-tailed hawk, a mountain bluebird, two rock doves.

At the porta-potties, the hikers disembarked. Dorothy passed out box lunches, and Lark gave the driver explicit instructions to be back around four-thirty that afternoon.

The first two miles of trail wound through pine, fir, and spruce forest and meandered along the shores of Alpine Creek, where yellow-flowered mimulus, better known as yellow monkey flowers, bloomed in profusion. The sun shone down brightly from a deep-blue sky. The air warmed to a comfortable temperature.

Lark set a leisurely pace, stopping to point out the birds. Broad-tailed hummingbirds, mountain chickadees, pygmy nuthatches, Townsend's solitaires, and pine siskins darted in and out among the trees. Several of the birders had lugged along scopes, and Lark allowed time to set up and focus on the various species.

A new volunteer spotted a three-toed woodpecker, and, ten minutes later, Owens spotted a pine grosbeak. They got lucky just before reaching the stream, when a blue grouse darted onto the path to dust itself.

Near the creek, Lark noticed an American dipper cavorting in the white water bubbling over the rocks. A lark-sized, mousy-gray bird, the dipper bobbed in jerky fashion, hiding behind the cascade, as though playing a game of hide-and-seek.

"Wait," Katherine said. "What's that?"

Two black birds on scimitar-shaped wings dove and wheeled overhead, then disappeared around the bend of the cliffs that ran along the other side of the creek.

"Black swifts."

The cry carried back along the line, and some of the stragglers hurried forward to see the aerialists in flight.

They hiked on, and around eleven o'clock, the walkie-talkie crackled to life. "Lark? Do you read me? Come in, Lark. Over."

"Hello, Dorothy." Lark had taken the lead, leaving Dorothy to bring up the rear.

"We have some tired folks back here. Is it about time to stop for lunch? Over."

"This isn't the Army," Cecilia said in the background.

"Hush."

Lark suppressed a laugh. "We're almost at the meadow. We can regroup there, and then I'll take any that want to go on. How does that sound?"

"Sounds good to me. Over and out."

It took nearly half an hour to assemble the group. Paul, Katherine, Norberto, and about six others had kept pace with Lark. Jan and Buzz lagged in the middle, and Dorothy and the rest straggled in behind. Lark gave everyone a chance to rest and eat his or her lunch, then asked who intended to climb to Paris Pond.

Paul, Katherine, Buzz, and six others raised their hands. Norberto raised his and tried pushing Jan's hand into the air.

"I can't, Norberto. I'm exhausted." She looked exhausted, too. Her blond hair hung limp around her shoulders. Mascara ringed her eyes. The crisp khaki birding outfit of the morning, no doubt courtesy of L.L. Bean's spring catalog, hung limp and wrinkled on her thin frame.

By contrast, Norberto looked sharp. His cargo pants still held their crease. Black boots matched a black T-shirt, and he'd tied a red-bandana burnoose around his head to ward off the sun. Decidedly foreign and dangerous looking, an allure that most women found irresistible. In fact, Lark had noticed that several of the volunteers let their eyes linger on Norberto, while favoring Jan with withering stares.

"You must come," insisted Norberto. "The job, remember?"

"It's really a sight to see from up there," cajoled Paul, looking natty in a turquoise jacket.

"Darn tootin', girl." Buzz sucked in a deep breath of mountain air and pounded his chest. "The exhilaration of the climb. We'll all help you."

Jan slumped down on a boulder. "Oh, all right. Give me a few more minutes to recuperate, and I'll try going a little ways. But I won't promise I won't turn back."

Lark gave her ten minutes, then insisted they bead out. "It's only another mile and a half, but the trail's steep, so it takes a while to hike up." She glanced at the sky. In the past several hours, puffy white clouds had started banding together to form billowing clouds with streaks of gray. "Elk Mountain attracts afternoon thunderstorms like a magnet. We still have time to make Paris Pond, but we don't want to dally."

She pressed them onward, this time taking the rear and waving good-bye to Dorothy, Cecilia, and Gertie.

"We'll be back in three hours." That would leave two hours to walk out to the bus.

The group crossed the creek on a narrow footbridge, then climbed quickly. The trail veered sharply left; below them, Alpine Meadow disappeared from view. Soon, sub-alpine fir and Engelmann spruce replaced the pine trees, then gave way to the elfin groves of krummholz that seized the land.

Before long, the path entered the tundra, a land of extremes, where strong winds and arctic temperatures radically shortened the growing season. The plants that grew here hugged the ground and sprouted protective coverings to shield themselves from the wind. Wildflowers such as snowball, saxifrage, anemone, sky pilot, and king's crown blanketed the spongy terrain. The climbers huddled into their jackets and bowed into the wind.

"It's in here that we might spot the white-tailed ptarmigan and the brown-capped rosy-finch," hollered Lark. "Keep your eyes open."

"Do you have any toothpicks?" Jan asked, walking in front of her.

"You're doing great," Buzz said, scooping his arm in hers and dragging her forward. "Just keep moving."

"Wait!" Jan stopped and pointed. "What's that?"

Mottled brown with a white underbelly, the bird stood frozen in place among a clump of rocks less than twenty-five feet from the path.

"That's the white-tailed ptarmigan." Paul crept forward, his binoculars trained on the bird. "Does everyone see it?"

Then, one of the special guest speakers pointed out a flock of brown-capped rosy-finches foraging several feet of the trail ahead.

"Both species. That's great. Now that everyone's seen them, how many of you want to go on?" Lark asked. The clouds had started closing in and were growing darker with each passing moment. "The trail climbs up there, crosses the ridge, and winds down to Paris Pond. The view is spectacular, but the weather looks iffy."

"I want to go on," Buzz said.

"Me, too," Paul said.

Katherine nodded.

Norberto prodded Jan. "We'll go, too. We've come this far."

Several of the others decided to turn back, but three of the volunteers chose to continue.

"Okay, then listen up. The rest of you start back down the trail. Everyone else, when we reach the pond, we're only going to have a few minutes." She glanced skyward. "When I give the signal, we'll need to head back."

"Let's move out, then." Buzz's enthusiasm overwhelmed her. Not only did he seem more energized as the day went on, he seemed more boisterous and enthusiastic. She wondered if the hike reminded him of his boot camp days and hoped he wouldn't start calling out time.

Left, left, left, right, left. I left my wife and forty-nine children alone in the woods in starving condition. Left, left.

With Norberto half-pulling, half-pushing, Jan made the crest of the ridge. The view opened before them. Paris Pond sparkled when parting clouds permitted the sunlight to pierce through, and Elk Park squatted in the valley below. Longs Peak rose majestically to their right, but it almost seemed as if they were as high as the summit.

"Oh, look. A hawk," Buzz said.

The bird glided on the thermals, circling, then swooping in search of prey along the pond's edge. A dark, rich brown, the golden wash on the bird's nape and head glittered in the sun.

"It's a golden eagle," corrected Lark.

"We've seen it. Now, can we go back?" Jan asked, plopping herself down on a rock.

"We have to hike down," Buzz said. "We've come this far."

"That argument worked on me earlier, but I'm not going any farther. I refuse to budge."

One of the remaining volunteers, a girl named Margo, stepped forward. "We've decided to head back. She can go with us."

"No. I'm not going anywhere right this minute. I need to rest." Jan huddled into her jacket and braced against the stiff breeze pouring over the lip of the mountain. "I'll wait here for the rest of you."

"It's apt to get cold," warned Lark. "At least go with the others as far as the tree line."

"I'm okay. I just need to sit," she said, waving them away.

"Suit yourself." Lark told the volunteers to head back, asking Margo to assure Dorothy and the others that the rest of them wouldn't be far behind. "Lead on, Buzz."

It took forty-five minutes to climb down to Paris Pond and back, and Lark kept expecting the walkie-talkie to crackle to life until she realized they were too far out of range for the signal to carry. To conserve the batteries, she turned it off. Cresting the ridge, they found Jan sitting on the same rock where they'd left her. She was shivering, her lips tinged slightly blue.

"Are you okay?" Buzz asked, sitting down beside her and rubbing his arm across her back.

"I'm freezing."

"Time to get up and move." Lark yanked Jan to her feet. Hypothermia was not uncommon, even in the summer, and sometimes all it took to trigger the warning signs was the combination of being tired and a chilly day. Lark chided herself for letting Jan sit there. She should have seen this coming. On the bright side, Jan didn't seem disoriented. Lark's bigger concern were the storm clouds moving in.

The thought conceived, a streak of lightning shot to the tundra, causing the hair on Lark's body to stand on end. The air around them crackled with static. The retort of thunder crashed around them.

"Time to move," she yelled. "Now!"

"What the...?" Jan cringed, burying her face in Buzz's shoulder.

"Shit." Norberto pushed Katherine ahead of him, starting her down the path. "Come on. We're sitting ducks up here."

The six of them scrambled down the hill as quickly as they could, Norberto propelling Katherine to move and Lark prodding Jan, Paul, and Buzz from behind. The lightning intensified.

Damn, why hadn't she paid closer attention to the storm, thought Lark. She had watched the clouds gathering as the storm had rolled in and stacked up behind the mountains. She knew the dangers of the Southwestern monsoons. She just thought they had time.

When they reached the krummholz, Lark breathed easier. At least there were trees here to draw the strikes, and the birders were no longer the tallest things spiking the landscape.

"Can we rest?" Jan asked, panting and scrambling for footing on the rocky trail.

"Just keep going," ordered Lark. "And tuck your binoculars inside your jacket."

The warning was barely issued before the rain started. A sprinkle of large drops pelted the ground, then the skies opened up, and the trail became a river of mud. Lark slipped, her ankle twisting beneath her. Falling, she landed full weight on her foot.

Ouch!

Lark tried pushing herself up, gingerly testing her weight on her ankle. A sharp stabbing pain shot up her calf.

Oh, man. Had she rebroken the darn thing?

Clambering to stand, she tried bearing her weight on her right foot again. This time the pain was less intense, and the ankle didn't buckle.

"Are you okay?" Paul asked, climbing back to where she

stood. Rain molded his hair to his head and streamed in rivulets off his face.

"I think I sprained my ankle. I'm hoping that's all I've done."

"Can you walk?"

"Do I have a choice?"

Chapter 14

It had taken them two hours to descend from the summit. The skies had opened in a gush of water, like God had turned on a faucet. After struggling along for a mile, they sat out the storm beneath a medium-sized boulder, watching the rain pummel the ground. Water puddled in low spots and eddied around stones on the path, creating small rivers of mud.

"Well, we needed the moisture," she said, attempting to lighten the mood, easing the weight off her aching ankle.

The only one with any humor left was Buzz. He drew in a breath and puffed out his chest. "What a bunch of sticks-in-the-mud. This rain just adds to the adventure."

"Stick a sock in it, Buzz." Jan tucked back a drippy strand of blond hair. "Look at us. We look like a soggy band of refugees."

After the rain let up, Lark led, limping her way out of the forest. Alpine Creek lay dead ahead. She could hear it rushing over the stones impeding its path.

Rushing! Not burbling like normal, but roaring like a technical river made only of rapids.

Reaching the willow tangles, she scanned the opposite bank, wondering where Dorothy and the others were. She yanked the walkie-talkie out of her pocket, turned it on, and hit the Talk button. "Dorothy, are you there?"

Two steps more, and she reached the path through the willows to the bridge. Rounding the corner, she stopped dead. The others plowed into her, like dominoes on the shove. Ahead of her, where the bridge crossed Alpine Creek, lay a chasm. The bank had washed away, leaving only a divot where the bridge had once been. The ground dropped away in a sheer wall.

"Where's the bridge?" Jan's hysterical voice pierced the summer afternoon. A yellow warbler flushed from a nearby bush.

Lark inched forward, gimping on her sore ankle, afraid that the land might fall away beneath her feet Against the opposite shore, the bridge lay collapsed and broken on the rocks.

"It looks like it's collapsed. We're not going to get back

across this way."

"Why not? We can climb down there," Buzz said.

"I don't think so," she said. "The ground's unstable. It's been undercut by water." Lark knew the trail. Upstream, the creek cascaded down a waterfall, too steep and slippery to traverse. Downstream, the creek ran below steep cliffs of granite. Without ropes and carabineers, they were stuck.

Turning up the volume on the walkie-talkie, she pressed the Talk switch and tried paging Dorothy again. "Come in, Dee. Where are you?"

"How can this be happening?" shrieked Jan. She raised her arms above her head, then slapping them hard against her sides, she whirled on Lark. "This is all your fault."

"Now calm down, little lady," Buzz said, stepping in between them. "Lark has no control over Mother Nature. We're talking mud slides here, probably caused by a flash flood. It happens, especially with a rain like the whopper we just rode out. The creek swells up, the current undercuts the bank, and the land above it scoots way. We're just lucky no one got hurt."

Jan glared at Buzz. "Who asked you?"

The radio crackled to life. "Come in, Lark. Over."

"Dorothy?" Relief flooded Lark's voice. "Where are you?"

"About a mile from the bus. With the rain, I decided we should go ahead and start back. Over."

Lark tamped down the feelings of abandonment welling up. "Look, we need help up here. The bridge is washed out."

"Repeat. Over."

"I said, the bridge is washed out. It's gone."

"Oh my," Cecilia said in the background.

A long silence followed.

"Dee, get the others down to the bus first, then send up some help."

"That's right, we're headed down to the bus. Over."

Lark slapped the radio against her hand and tried again. "Send help."

"I copy. Over."

The radio protocol was killing her. "Did Margo and the others catch up to you, yet?"

"Yes, they're here. Over."

"Good." One less thing to worry about. "Do me a favor?"

"Ask them to bring a helicopter," Jan said.

"Hurry!"

"Ten four. We're about an hour from the bus. Over and out." Dorothy clicked out, and Lark turned off the walkie-talkie to conserve the batteries. It was after four, and the sun was dropping behind Elk Mountain, casting long shadows across the meadow and valley floor. The clouds swirled back in on a strong wind, dropping a steady drizzle.

Jan and Norberto retreated to the rocks with Katherine. Buzz ambled off on a mission, determined to find a way out. Lark hunkered down in the shelter of a small pine tree next to Paul.

"If the winds don't let up, they're not going to get a crew in here tonight, much less a helicopter."

"That's what I was thinking." Worry lines etched deep in Paul's forehead, crow's feet crinkled around his eyes.

Lark scribbled an SOS in the mud. "I think we should tell the others to be prepared to spend the night."

"Before you do that, we have to talk."

"About what?"

"I know why Esther was killed."

Lark's pulse quickened. "You do?"

"Yes." Paul glanced around furtively, then lowered his voice. "She told me she was going to blow the lid off the Jitters operation during her closing speech this coming Thursday. She said she had proof of a scam involving the company. I didn't believe her. I thought she was angry over Katherine's courting of Jan Halloway." Paul leaned forward, making sure they were still alone. "When you brought up the ledger at dinner, I realized I was wrong, and she was telling me the truth. I need to look at the ledger." His eyes narrowed. "You still have it, don't you?"

She decided not to tell him the ledger had been stolen during the break-in. Though, for all she knew, he might have taken it. This could be one giant ruse, an elaborate fishing expedition designed to ferret out how much she knew. Paranoia aside, she couldn't help feeling that she'd just been stranded on a remote hillside with a killer. "How would Chipe's records provide information that would harm Jitters in any way?"

"The numbers in the ledger blow the cover on the coffee wars."

"The coffee wars? You mean as in competition between the coffee companies, or as in the conflict between the coffee growers and the PRI?"

"Both. If she has the information I think she has, the numbers recorded are way too high."

Lark still had no clue what he was talking about, except she, too, had realized the numbers were off. "I found something else I'd like to ask you about," she said, steering the subject away from the missing ledger. "A letter you wrote to Esther, dated a couple of years ago."

He covered his face with his hands. "So you know?"

"I know you were in love with her." The words tasted bitter, like an admission of guilt. Reading other people's mail was not just a federal crime, it was a mortal sin.

"It's true. Two years ago, we were both in Chiapas on business. It happened."

"Did Vic find out?"

"I don't think so, but Katherine did. She was dead set against Esther's and my relationship from the beginning, and she had the power to end it."

"How so?"

"She has the money. She is Migration Alliance."

"You gave up the love of your life for a job?"

"It's not just a job to me. I've worked a lifetime to get where I am. Even Esther wasn't worth giving up my dreams."

"That's sad."

"You think I killed her, don't you?" His tone was edgy. "How could you possibly believe that? Tell me, why would I murder the woman I loved?"

Loved being the operative word. Lark steeled herself against the pain in his voice. "Money?"

"I don't need any money. I have Katherine." The bitterness in the words overshadowed his anguish. Paul picked up a pine needle and carved a white-line heart on his skin. "After Katherine found out about Esther and me, there was an ugly scene. Katherine laid down an ultimatum. I had a choice: Esther, or Migration Alliance and the position of executive director. I'd worked so hard. But, then, so had Katherine. Her father had provided the seed money, but Katherine worked tirelessly to find ways to increase the wealth of the organization in order to insure its work continue. We worked together, as a team. She was so possessive, you'd have thought we were married instead of just partners." He drew a squiggly line through the heart. "But ours was a commitment and a union that couldn't be broken. Esther understood that and left."

"And Vic never found out?"

"It was six months later Esther and Vic moved in together. I don't think he ever knew about me. If I'd asked her to, she would have left him. It would have killed him." Paul looked up, pain reflected in his eyes and face. "The truth be told, he loved her more than I did."

Lark felt no empathy for Paul. For the sake of prestige, he'd squandered love. "What can I say?"

"Hey, it's life." Paul threw down the pine needle. "And nothing's changed. You need to keep your eyes open. Whoever killed Esther knows you've seen the ledger, and—"

A cracking of branches from upstream announced Buzz's arrival, interrupting their conversation. Standing at the edge of the trees, he swept crumbled branches from his flattop and off the shoulders of his jacket. "There's no way out of there, folks," announced Buzz. "Not in either direction."

"I could have told you that," grumbled Lark, moving out into the clearing.

"Told us what?" asked Norberto, pushing through the bushes behind her. Where had he come from?

"That there's no way across the creek, either upstream or down," she said, recovering quickly. "And it's starting to get late. I think we have to accept the fact that we may have to spend the night up here."

"Hoo boy," groaned Buzz.

"I'll try reaching Dorothy again for their ETA, but…" She let the inference speak for itself.

Norberto turned back toward the overhang. "Jan can't stop

shaking."

"Then we need to build a fire to get her dry."

Buzz and Norberto headed out in search of fuel. Lark sent Paul back to check on Jan. He seemed only too happy to oblige. Lark fiddled with the controls on the walkie-talkie and finally got through.

"Dorothy, did you get a call for help through?"

"That's affirmative. It's on the way, over."

"Dee, cut the over stuff, and just talk to me. I'm worried Jan Halloway's developed a case of hypothermia. We need to get her off this mountain. Just tell me what's going on."

"Because of the wind and nightfall, Mountain Search and Rescue can't get a helicopter up to you until morning. Then there's no place to land it on your side of the Alpine Creek. The storm washed out the trail in spots, so it's too treacherous to hike up in the dark. They're talking about coming up in the morning."

"Ten four," Lark said. "Over and out."

Lark's survival skills were rusty, going back twenty years to her Girl Scout days. Buzz's were honed to perfection. In no time flat, he'd collected enough dry brush and kindling to start a small fire. Norberto produced some matches, and the two men fanned the flames.

In the meantime, Lark pulled a dry sweatshirt out of her backpack and peeled Jan out of her wet clothing.

"Put this on."

"I'm fine." Jan tried pushing Lark's hand away, but her own hand missed.

"You're not fine," Lark said, unzipping Jan's wet jacket. Underneath, her shirt was soaked and plastered against her skin. "How's your vision?"

"Fine," Jan said, rubbing her eyes. "I can see perfectly, except for the smoke."

Norberto chuckled, watching them with amusement. His cargo pants were now stained with soot, and his black T-shirt whitened with ash, but the grungier he got, the better he looked. And more dangerous, in a Pierce Brosnan sort of way.

"Don't just stand there enjoying the show," Lark said. "Help me."

Together, they stripped Jan down to her bra and forced her arms into the sleeves of the dry sweatshirt. As Norberto's dark eyes strayed to her breasts, Lark yanked the sweatshirt into place, cutting off the view.

Norberto grinned. "You can't blame a guy."

With Jan bundled up in warmer garments, Lark assessed their supplies. Between the six of them, they had four bottles of water and a granola bar stuffed deep in Lark's pack. She couldn't vouch for how long it had been there, but they didn't need food to survive the night.

Shelter was the critical thing. Even though the rain had abated, lightning flashes high on the mountain indicated the storm wasn't over. Lark glanced up at the darkening sky. "You know, if we want to stay dry, we need to build a shelter."

Buzz jumped into gear. "She's right. If we get some stout logs we can construct—"

Paul cut him off. "She said shelter, not cabin."

"No, he's right, Paul. If we can find some long branches, we can cut boughs and tie them in place to form a wall to lean up against the overhang."

Paul looked skeptical. "What are we going to tie them up with?"

"How about shoelaces?" Buzz said.

"What are we going to cut the branches with?"

Lark produced a Swiss Army knife. "It has a saw blade."

By ten o'clock, the makeshift wall stood in place, and the inside of the Swiss Family Robinson–type shelter felt almost cozy. They had lashed together a wall of tree limbs and boughs strong enough to shield them from the threatening wind and rain. Prying her boots off at last, Lark leaned back against a rock, stretched her legs out in front of her, and dried her socks by the fire. Her ankle throbbed.

"I have a question," Jan said. Wearing Lark's blue sweatshirt with her blond hair curling around her ears, she looked like high school cheerleader at a woodsy. "Where does someone go to the bathroom?"

Lark pointed toward the woods.

"In the dark? By myself?"

A walk in the forest alone in the dark wasn't Lark's idea of a picnic, either. If only she didn't feel responsible for the predicament they were in. "Let me put my boots back on, and I'll go with you."

"I'll go, too," Katherine offered.

"Isn't one baby-sitter enough?" Buzz asked. "Or is it a woman thing?"

"Stuff a stock in it, Buzz," Jan said, allowing Norberto to help her to her feet. "And don't think we're saying nice things about you."

On his snort, Lark stepped around the makeshift wall into the stark moonlight. Without laces, the heels of her boots slipped up and down. Too much walking, and she would have blisters come morning. Turning her back on the campfire, she stepped off the path and headed into the woods. "We don't have to go far. We can duck behind these trees over here."

"What do we wipe with?" Jan asked.

"Pine needles." Katherine rolled her eyes at Lark over the top of Jan's head.

"You're joking, right?"

"The other choice is to drip dry," explained Lark.

Jan groaned. "I'd have made a lousy pioneer."

They peed without any more talk, then headed back toward camp, single file. The storm had left the vegetation moist. Moonlight sparkled off the willows and danced along the creek. Closer to camp, the fire shed warm inviting light on the path. Katherine hurried ahead, but Jan hung back, something obviously on her mind.

"I want to thank you for saving my life, Lark."

"Let's not be overly dramatic," Lark said, uncomfortable with the praise. "All I did was make you put on a dry sweatshirt."

"If you hadn't forced me, I might have frozen to death. And I know the fire was your idea, and the shelter. I'd like to reward you somehow. If there's anything I can—"

"Nothing," Lark said, cutting her off. "Your thanks is more than enough."

Lark awakened at dawn when the first rays of sun peeked over the top of the mountain, smacking her full in the face. Rolling on the hard ground, she pushed herself up on her elbow, brushing dirt and pine needles out of the top of her hair. The end was still braided, but Lark imagined it looked worse for the wear.

The others were all still asleep. Katherine, curled near the fire, her dark head crooked on one arm, looked like a porcelain doll. Jan, scrunched up fetus-like beside Norberto, looked cold. Buzz lay flat on his back, his head propped on a bed of pine needles, snoring lightly.

Where was Paul? she wondered. He must have gotten up to go pee.

Not a bad idea. Lark sat up and stretched, feeling the pressure of her own bladder. The sky was clear, and the air smelled fresh. Reaching down, she gingerly rubbed her ankle. Her foot wasn't too swollen this morning. That was a good sign. Clambering to her feet, she eased her weight onto her right foot. Tender, but usable.

Lark worked her feet into her boots, then hobbled out from under the lean-to. Turning toward the woods, she gimped her way up the path, breathing deep of the mountain air. Dew sparkled on the leaves, and a yellow-rumped warbler sang from the trees.

At the bend in the trail, Lark stepped off the path and moved deeper into the forest The underbrush crackled beneath her feet. A flash of turquoise in the woods to her right pulled her up short. "Paul?"

There was no mistaking his bright-colored jacket. He sat on the ground, leaning against a tree. He appeared to be watching something. Probably a bird.

"Did you spot something interesting?" she whispered, working her way quietly up behind him. "Paul?"

Reaching out her hand, she touched his shoulder, half expecting him to jump. Instead, he slumped sideways.

"Paul?"

She shook him, and his head lolled to the right. His eyes matched the color of his turquoise jacket. They stared sightlessly at the morning sun.

Chapter 15

A red stain spread across the front of Paul's jacket, turning the turquoise purple. An angry gash gouged deep in his neck. Nearby lay a red-handled Swiss Army knife.

Her knife. The one she'd lent him to cut boughs with.

A scream bubbled up. Not a squeaky scream, but a full-throated screech that caused a flock of pine siskin to flush from the trees, and something larger to crash away through the undergrowth.

Lark clamped her hands across her mouth and tried breathing slowly through her nose, forcing herself to calm down.

Was he really dead? He looked dead.

She reached out a tentative hand, touching his wrist to feel for a pulse. His flesh felt cold, like precooked liver.

Panic bubbled up again. It looked like someone had slashed his throat.

Slowly, she backed away from his body; then she turned and ran toward the trail. With every step, sharp pains radiated up from her ankle. A dull throb pulsed in her temple. The underbrush on the forest floor clawed at her feet, tripping her. The branches on the bushes and trees snagged her clothes, stinging and scratching her face as she pushed through the woods toward the narrow path. Her heart pounded, and she gasped for air.

Reaching the trail, she took several faltering steps, then stopped and threw up in the bushes. Bile burned the back of her throat, and she vomited in spasms. Then, with her stomach emptied, she screamed for help.

"Buzz! Somebody! Get up!"

Ignoring the shooting pains in her leg and head, Lark sprinted for the clearing. She heard Buzz growling to life behind the lean-to.

"What's going on? Who's yelling?"

"It sounds like Lark," Katherine said. "Paul? Where's Paul?"

The shelter loomed in sight, and Lark slowed her pace. The sound of Katherine's voice had pierced through her panic, sobering her to the reality of the situation. Katherine was Paul's partner. The rest of them were Paul's friends. One of them was Paul's murderer.

"What's wrong?" demanded Buzz, stepping out in to the open and grabbing her by the shoulders. "Did something scare you?"

Lark glanced at the others, then looked at the ground. "Can I talk to you a minute, Buzz?"

Katherine's eyes grew round with alarm. "Did something happen? Was Paul with you?"

Damn! Lark scrunched her eyes closed.

"Where is he?" she demanded. "He was with you, wasn't he?"

"He's…" Lark looked at Buzz. "I found him…" She turned back to Katherine. "He's dead."

A shocked silence ensued.

"Dead?" Jan whispered.

"You must be wrong," Katherine said, her black hair swinging around her face. "You can't be right."

"I don't know what happened. I found him leaning against a tree. His throat was slashed."

"Where is he?" demanded Katherine, heading for the trail.

"He's back in the woods," Lark gestured lamely. "But I don't think it's a good idea—"

"I don't really care what you think," Katherine said. "How could you just leave him out there?"

Lark blocked her path. "Katherine, he's dead."

"And what if he's not?" Katherine pushed Lark aside with a strength that knocked her off balance. She turned to Buzz.

"You have to stop her."

Lark felt another wave of nausea and dropped her head to her knees. "And someone needs to get the sheriff up here."

Buzz hesitated for a moment before charging after Katherine. "Lark's right," he said, forcing her back to the clearing. "It's better if we all stay here until the sheriff arrives."

"What are you talking about? Someone besides her needs to go check on him. What if she's wrong? What if he's still alive and bleeding to death? Minutes can make the difference."

Katherine cast about for support. "Are the rest of you just going to take her word for it?"

Lark straightened. "Are you saying I would lie about something like this?"

Katherine stepped to within nose-touching distance and shrieked on the morning breeze, "Why not? You're the one that got us stranded up here in the first place. You're the one who gave him the knife. You're the one he confided in."

"Confided in? What are you talking about, Katherine?" Jan asked.

"Enough!" Buzz roared. "Everybody, sit down."

Lark waited for Katherine to move away, then hobbled over to the boulder outcropping and sat on a relatively flat piece of rock. While the others banded together under the overhang, the sharp granite poked against Lark's rear end, bringing the proverbial "pain in the ass" to life.

"Katherine is right," Buzz said. "Someone else needs to go check on Paul." He glanced at Lark. "Just to make sure. You understand. And, we need to reach Dorothy MacBean and have her notify the sheriff and park officials. Where is the walkie-talkie?"

Lark patted her jacket pockets. The handheld radio was gone. "I had it right here last night."

"Do you remember having it this morning?"

"No. I didn't use it. Maybe it fell out of my pocket while I was sleeping?" Lark started searching the flat spot where she'd woken. Norberto joined her, and together they combed the area.

"I don't see it," he said finally.

Katherine whispered something to Jan, then glared at Lark.

"Geez," Buzz said, slapping the palm of his hand against his forehead. "Think, Lark."

"Like I told you, I had it last night."

After a hasty search of the clearing turned up no sign of the walkie-talkie, Buzz called them back together. "What we need is a plan. Here's the way I see this operation. First, Lark, Norberto, and I will go back to where Lark found Paul." Katherine sputtered a protest, but Buzz held up his hand and silenced her. "If he's alive, if, Norberto and I can carry him out.

Lark knows where he is."

Katherine turned and buried her head against Jan's shoulder. Jan smoothed the woman's hair. "Go. We're okay here."

Limping in the lead, Lark backtracked her way through the forest, past the area where she heaved, to the spot where she'd turned into the woods. Several yards in from the path, they found Paul's body.

Buzz crouched, creeping forward like a Russian Cossack dancer. "He's dead, all right We'd better not touch anything more."

A crackle of static broke the air.

Norberto ducked, then glanced around. "What was that? Did anyone else hear that?"

"Lark? Come in, Lark. Over." Dorothy's voice sounded muffled. Out of reflex, Lark patted her jacket pockets.

Buzz levered Paul's body. The walkie-talkie lay beneath him, pressed into the ground. "How the hell did this get here?"

What was Paul doing with the walkie-talkie? He had to have lifted it off Lark while she was sleeping. Had he been trying to contact someone?

Norberto squatted down and whispered something to Buzz. He replied in the same hushed tones.

"What are you two discussing?"

Neither man answered. Buzz looked at the ground.

"You don't think I had anything to do with this?" She felt an urge to defend herself, then decided better of it. No sense in adding fuel to the fire.

"Let's go back to camp," Buzz said. He squeezed past Lark, pushing a branch out of his way and letting it snap back in her face.

Lark caught the branch in her hand. "You didn't answer my question, Major."

Buzz turned to face her. "Little lady, I don't know what to think. All I know for sure is that that man back there is dead."

No shit, Sherlock.

"It was your knife, and everyone connected to you and your coffee business seems to be dropping like flies."

She felt an irrational urge to giggle, while tears of anger

154

burned her eyes. How dare he accuse her of murdering Paul? "For the record, if one of us killed him, it wasn't me."

"Lark? Come in, Lark." Dorothy's voice crackled over the radio again. "Are you there? Over."

"Oh my, I hope they're all right," Cecilia said in the background.

Buzz keyed the walkie-talkie. "This is Major Buzz Aldefer. Over."

"Thank heavens, we were beginning to get worried." Relief flooded Dorothy's voice. "Search and Rescue's on the way. Over."

"Ten four," Buzz said. "And you better call the Sheriff's Department. Paul Owens is dead. Over."

There was an answering crackle as the microphone was keyed on Dorothy's end, but no voice came through.

"Do you copy? Over."

"Ten four," Dorothy said. "I'll contact Sheriff Garcia. Over and out."

The search party arrived in the meadow within the hour. Lark was glad to see Eric and Harry among the rescuers.

"Hey," Eric said, standing on one leg, the other knee cocked. Except for being fully clothed, he made a perfect Abercrombie & Fitch photo opportunity.

"Hey, yourself."

"We heard you had some trouble last night."

Word spread fast.

"Are you okay?"

"Better now."

"Glad to hear it," Harry said.

Eric nodded in agreement, and Lark felt warmer inside. Brushing back the loose hairs that strayed from her braid, she crossed her arms in front of her chest. "Did Dorothy get a hold of Vic?"

"Ian contacted him by radio. He's on his way." Eric paused. "Bernie's en route, too, with the federal boys."

Paul was murdered on Forest Service land, so park law enforcements personnel would have to check out the scene of the crime. It was a guaranteed circus.

"Listen up," yelled Ian Ogburn, a U.S. Fish and Wildlife officer and head of the local Mountain Search and Rescue team. He clapped his hands to get everyone's attention. "This is what we're going to do."

The plan hatched was to build a zip line using a rope and pulley-type device.

Tying the backpack full of beef jerky, Gatorade, and granola bars on the end of a thick rope, Ian twirled it lasso-style above his head and heaved it across the chasm. Buzz scrambled to pick it up.

"One of you needs to tie the rope in that tree," said Ian, pointing high in the branches of a giant ponderosa. It sat a good ten feet back from the creek, its trunk measuring over six feet in circumference. The closest limbs to the ground jutted out from eight feet in the air. "Which one of you knows how to tie a bowline knot?"

Lark and Buzz both raised their hands. A bowline was a strong knot forming a loop that didn't slip. She'd learned to tie one sailing summers off the coast of Maine.

"One of you needs to shinny up there, wrap your end of the rope around the tree about fifteen feet in the air, and tie off. Any questions?"

Since it required a leg up to perform the feat, Buzz cupped his hands and offered to lever Lark into the tree. "I've got sixty pounds on you. There's no way you and Norberto together could boost me high enough."

"Promise you'll add monkey to my list of accomplishments?"

"Let's go on three. One, two…" Buzz strained, boosting her into the air. Lark grabbed hold of the lowest branch, swinging on the limb like a child on a jungle gym bar. Pushing against the bark with her feet, she shinnied up into the tree.

"Go a little higher," Ian yelled.

Grabbing the branch above her, Lark hauled herself farther up into the tree. Fifteen feet below, the ground swayed.

"Don't look down," Buzz ordered.

"Got it," Lark said, focusing her gaze on the branches above her. There would be plenty of time for looking down when she tried climbing out of the tall pine.

Two branches higher, and Ian yelled, "There, that's high enough."

Lark wrapped the end of the rope around the thick tree trunk. Making a loop in the long side of the rope, she fed the end up, around, back, and yanked down. The knot tightened and held. She tugged. "Okay. It's tied off."

Ian jerked on the tope. "Is it holding?"

She flashed him a thumbs-up.

"Okay, climb down."

That was easier said than done.

Lark stretched her leg out, searching with her toe for a branch to rest her foot on. Slowly, she inched her way down the tree, until her foot met air.

"That's as far as you can go," Buzz called. "You'll have to jump down from there."

"Jump?" Not with her ankle throbbing like it was, and her head still tender. "Can't you reach up and get me?"

"You're still too high. Try hanging from one of the branches, like you did when you climbed up there?"

Lark peered down at Buzz, and the world spun. Now she knew why she'd never been a mountain climber. Clutching the tree, she pressed her face against the trunk. Sticky, pine-scented sap oozed across her cheek.

"Okay, here goes." Securing herself between two branches, she worked her way into a sitting position on the lowest one. "Be ready to catch me in case this doesn't work."

Flipping onto her stomach, she swayed in the air, then spun over the top and dropped into a hanging position. Tree bark scraped her stomach and the palms of the hands.

"Slick move," shouted Eric.

"It wasn't intentional."

"You're right above me, Lark. Let go, and I'll catch you."

"Doesn't this remind you of one of those management retreat activities?" Jan asked, speaking for the first time. "You know, where they ask you to trust each other and make you play dumb games, like the one where you fall into the arms of the other managers." She laughed. "I always knew they'd drop me."

157

Luckily for Lark, Buzz caught her before she hit the ground.

Soon, Ian and several of the rescue crew zipped across the chasm using special carabineers. They quickly set up a pulley system designed to transport people back across in a sling.

The first one to go was Katherine. Jan followed, then Norberto. On each return trip, a law enforcement officer descended upon Elk Mountain. Before long, the clearing swarmed with officers. Then, once again, Lark escorted them to the spot where she'd first found Paul.

Hours had passed since she'd last been there. The sun had warmed the land, heating the forest, stirring the insects to life. Flies buzzed around Paul's body, flitting across his jacket and nibbling at his blue-tinged lips.

"He's dead, all right," Crandall said, sitting back on his haunches and pushing his fingers through his hair. "Looks like someone wanted him dead." He turned to Buzz. "It would take someone pretty big to subdue a man this size."

Vic stroked his mustache. "Not necessarily, Bernie."

"Why do you say that?" Crandall scootched forward. "What am I missing here?"

Lark's legs felt weak, and she propped herself up against a nearby tree.

Vic reached out, and with one finger pushed Paul's face to the side. "See this?" He pointed to a lump above Paul's right ear. "He took a blow to the head."

"Now hold on a minute, boys," Buzz said. The older man looked flustered. "Who's to say he didn't fall? Maybe he bumped his head, then landed on the knife? There's rocks all over the place."

Vic shook his head. "There's no way he could have sat up on his own after pumping out that much blood. Nope," he dusted his hands against his knees, and stood. "It looks like our friend here was helped out of this world. I'll put money on it."

"Guess this sort of lets Vic and Teresa off the hook," Lark said.

Crandall turned, raising his eyebrows. "How do you figure, Drummond?"

"Neither one of them could have killed Paul. They were stuck

158

on the other side of the creek."

"That's true, Drummond, but it doesn't let them off the hook for Esther's murder."

"You're saying there are two killers? That someone else murdered Paul?"

"It's possible. Maybe there's two of them working together." Crandall rose to his feet. "Of course, if you were to eliminate them, it sort of narrows down the suspect list, don't it, Drummond?"

And now there were five.

Chapter 16

Lark leaned against the trunk of an aspen tree and tried spit-washing the sap off her face. Thirty feet away, the Search and Rescue team wrestled to transport the stretcher carrying Paul Owens's body across the gorge.

First Esther, now Paul. If he had been right, Esther died because she planned to blow the lid on some illicit Mexican-based operation. Which meant he had died for the same reason. But why?

Lark figured it must have to do with the numbers in the ledger. He had said the numbers were too high.

"Lark, you're next," shouted Ian.

She walked to the edge of the washout, stepped into the harness, and allowed Ian to tighten the belt around her waist. Then he clipped the harness to the transport strap.

"Have you ever ridden a zip line?"

"Nope."

"Are you afraid of heights?"

"A little." More so since her climbing accident. Even climbing a tree had brought on a feeling of vertigo. It swept over her now in spite of the fact her feet were planted solidly on the ground. A déjà vu of sorts, or a sympathetic memory, like men who experience pregnancy with their wives.

"Then take my advice. Don't look down."

Lark cheated, sneaking a look at the washout and creek below. The ground dropped away. The world spun. She closed her eyes and gripped the rope with both hands, then Ian shoved her into the air.

Two hours later, snuggled down into a hot tub of water, Lark was grateful to be home. The soap bubbles stung her cuts and scrapes, but the water warmed her to the bone, and for the first time in over twenty-four hours, she felt human again.

"Let me get this straight," Rachel said. She perched on the closed commode, having shown up within hours of the rescue for the official word on "the ordeal on Elk Mountain." Dorothy and Cecilia had tendered their own versions, but both were prone to embellishment. "So you're saying Vic and Teresa have been exonerated?"

"In my opinion, though technically, until the two murders are officially linked, they're both still suspects in Esther's murder."

"For the sake of argument, let's throw them out. That leaves five suspects."

"Four, please. I swear, I didn't do it."

"Four, then." Rachel ticked them off on her fingers. "Buzz, Katherine, Jan, and Norberto."

"Bingo."

She recounted. "Bing. There is no O unless you add yourself back in."

Lark threw a shower sponge at Rachel, then slipped beneath the mounds of bubbles to wet her hair. She worked her fingers through the tresses, fanning them out until the long blond strands swayed like seaweed on the water.

Out of the four, Lark had whittled the field to three. Resurfacing, she used her hands to squeegee the water and soap from her face, then said, "For what it's worth, I don't think Katherine did it."

"Why not?"

"No reason, just a gut feeling. You should have seen her reaction when she learned Paul was dead."

"She might be a good actress. She's had a lot of public speaking experience."

"But what would have been her motive?"

"Didn't you say she forced the breakup between Esther and Paul? Maybe she wanted Esther out of the picture for good."

"Why? The affair happened over two years ago, and Paul chose the Alliance. If she'd wanted to kill her, why wait so long? Two years goes way beyond premeditation. And, besides, Esther was no longer a threat." Lark tamped down a mound of bubbles. "Let's abandon emotion as a motive and look at the facts. Both victims were connected to the Chipe Coffee Company. Let's suppose the reason for the murders was financial, that it all had to do with business. Bad business."

Silence blanketed the room.

Finally, when it grew uncomfortable, Rachel spoke. "Then you could be in danger." She crossed her legs and leaned back against the toilet tank. "How much did you tell Bernie and Vic?"

"I told them everything."

"Did you tell them about the letter from Paul?"

"No." She had intended to tell Crandall about the letter she'd found, but had never gotten the chance. "Vic was there the whole time, and I didn't want to upset him." Groping for a towel, she dried her face. "You know something, Rae?"

"What?"

"I never fished the letter I kept out of the hamper."

Rachel went in search of the envelope in the khaki shorts, while Lark climbed out of the bath, toweled dry, and assessed her injuries in the bathroom mirror. There wasn't a square inch on her body that remained unbruised. Even her hair hurt. Pulling on clean blue jeans and a fresh T-shirt, she let her hair hang loose and padded barefoot to the kitchen.

The mess from last night was in remission. The books shoved haphazardly back in the bookcases, the drawers closed, the cereal swept up, and the counters wiped down. Lark guessed Rachel had been busy. She heard the washing machine click on and begin to fill, then Rachel emerged from the laundry room, letter in hand.

"Sit," she said, handing Lark the envelope. "You read this, while I make some grilled cheese sandwiches."

Too tired to argue, and glad to have someone taking care of her for a change, Lark obeyed. Pulling the letter out of the envelope, she skimmed the page.

"Well?"

"It doesn't say much. Lots of mush. But he does apologize for the blowup with Katherine, so I guess that part of the story was true." She read on. "Can you believe this, he actually asks her to wait for him."

"Bastard."

Lark glanced up. Whatever Rachel was thinking, Lark bet it involved her soon-to-be-ex-husband, Roger. She was slicing cheese with a vengeance, thin shoulders tensed, biceps taut. Tears had formed at the corners of her eyes, and she blotted them away with her sleeve.

"That crying stuff's reserved for onions," Lark said. She stuffed the letter back in the envelope and tossed it on the table. Time to change the subject. "Do you know what else is weird?"

"What?"

"Buzz Aldefer could not identify a golden eagle."

Rachel slathered butter on the back sides of the bread and plopped them into a pan. "Sorry, Lark, but I don't see what IDing birds has to do with the price of coffee in Mexico."

"The guy's billed as a big government birdwatcher. He's been a Hawkwatch volunteer in Chiapas. So why couldn't he name that bird? A golden eagle isn't a hard identification to make. Not if you know eagles. Heck, even you could do that."

Rachel flashed her a bright smile. "I'll take that as a compliment."

"Trust me," Lark said. "That man is no birdwatcher."

Rachel grabbed a spatula and flipped the sandwiches. "I don't mean to harp at you," she said, cranking the heat on the stove, "but why haven't you called your dad and asked him to check out Buzz Aldefer?"

The question caught her off guard. "Because."

"That's not an answer."

"Because, asking Senator Nathan Drummond, the senior senator from Connecticut, for a favor means owing him big time. Nothing ever comes free. The price varies, but there's always a price."

In the Drummond household, even love came on condition. It had been doled out for good grades and nice behavior, and it had taken her a long time to realize that she'd spent most of her life bartering for affection. "I already owe him for the phone call I made in June to find out about Forest Nettleman."

The phone call had paid off. Through her father's connections, they'd discovered that Nettleman, the soon-to-be ex-U.S. Representative from Colorado's Fourth District, had been an ecowarrior in his younger days—information important to solving the murder of Donald Bursau. But it had come with a price.

"Believe me," continued Lark. "One of these days my father

will call in the chit."

Rachel withheld comment, serving up lightly burned toasted cheese sandwiches. They munched in silence. Rachel drank water. Lark guzzled milk. Finally, Lark couldn't take any more.

"Okay, if I call, Rae. Mind you, I said, if, what do I ask him?"

Rachel broke her sandwich in half and twirled oozing melted cheddar around her finger. "I'd ask him if he's ever heard of Buzz Aldefer, or if he knows anyone in the top brass of the U.S. Air Force who can verify Buzz's military presence in Mexico. Surely he'd check it out for you."

"Even if he did, he'll just come back and say he doesn't know anything." Lark wiped a milk mustache off on her napkin. "He's not stupid. The U.S. can't admit any knowledge of government activity in Mexico. They're our allies. Besides, I'm sure his phones are tapped."

"Then ask him to call you back from the pay phone on the corner. It'll drive the surveillance team wild."

Lark laughed. "You love this cloak and dagger stuff, don't you?"

"No! It's just how they do it in the movies."

"Get real. Admit it. You love it."

Rachel shook her head and started loading the dishwasher. "He's your father, Lark. What's the worst that can happen?"

Out of excuses, Lark placed the call. The conversation with her father was brief. He was headed out to a "function," but he would check things out and call her back.

"Well, I've got to go," Rachel said, wiping her hands on a dish towel as Lark hung up the phone. "There's an EPOCH meeting at Bird Haven in an hour."

Monday. Lark had forgotten all about the meeting. "Maybe I should come—"

"Maybe you should take a nap."

Rae had a point. Every muscle in her body ached. "I guess you're right."

"Of course, I'm right. You're as bad as Katherine Saunders."

"What's that supposed to mean?"

"Dorothy told me that Katherine showed up at the conference headquarters this afternoon and announced that the show would go on. Apparently, she's decided to give the workshops as planned because, 'Paul would have wanted it that way.' Gag." Rachel pulled on her jacket and scooped up the keys to her car. "I'll call you tomorrow. Meanwhile, get some rest."

"Hey, Rae?" Lark out called following Rachel out onto the porch and watching her scamper to the bottom of the steps. She paused, one foot in the car.

"Hey, what?"

"Thanks."

"De nada."

Lark sat down on the porch steps and watched until the green Toyota disappeared from sight. Trusting people came hard, and most people she met didn't care to fight through the veneer of self-sufficiency she threw in their path. Rachel, on the other hand, had leapt the hurdles.

Tipping her face toward the sun, Lark basked in the warmth of the rays and soaked in the scenery. Longs Peak and Elk Mountain rose in the distance beyond the Drummond like two giant siblings come out to play. They wore snowfield hats with pointy pompadours, and the afternoon sun shimmered off cliff faces positioned like well-aligned teeth. Idyllic and deadly.

But it wasn't the mountain that had killed Paul Owens. A person of flesh and blood had ended his life. And now, two people, both of whom were connected to the Chipe Coffee Company, were dead. The question was, why? Because of what they knew?

Possibly.

More likely, it was because of what they planned to tell.

It was still dark when Lark woke up.

Her heart pounded, and she lay still, barely breathing, trying to orient herself to her surroundings. Slivers of moonlight crept in around the edges of the curtains. She lay on top of a comforter, in her clothes.

She remembered moving from the deck to the bedroom and nothing more. Now, except for the person standing at the foot of her bed watching her sleep, she was completely alone.

A dark figure.

Her heart banged in her chest, and she feigned slumber, fighting off shivers of fear. Adrenaline pumped through her veins, and she willed herself to lie still.

Who was it? Who was standing there? The killer?

She didn't dare open her eyes any further for fear the moonlight shimmering across her face would give her away. Her muscles twitched. Lark shifted positions and pretended to stretch in her sleep.

The figure remained rooted in place, like a mannequin posed at the foot of the bed.

Panic welled up inside her, and she stuffed it back down, trying to remember whether she'd locked the doors before lying down on the bed. The memory eluded her.

Stupid. That was the first thing she should have done.

A warm hand touched her foot. Lark's heart leaped to her throat, threatening to choke her.

"Lark. Wake up." The voice belonged to Teresa Cruz.

Lark leaped out of bed, banging her ankle on the bedside table. "What in the hell are you doing in here?"

She flipped on the bedside lamp, bathing the room in a soft warm glow, then reached to massage her ankle bone. Teresa stepped back. Her dress—the same outfit she'd worn to sing in—hung in tatters on her tiny frame. One of her eyes was swollen black and blue. A green tinge radiated out from the center in painted streaks of yellow. She licked a cut on her swollen lower lip and drew a ragged breath.

"Oh my God, what happened to you?"

"He tried to rape me."

"Who?" Lark searched her face. "Jacobs?"

Teresa nodded, ducking her head in shame.

Lark's blood percolated. "Where is he now?"

"At the Manor House. He came back to get his paycheck, and…" She dropped her chin. "I had nowhere to go."

"Sit," ordered Lark, pointing to the bed. She reached for the phone. "I'm calling Bernie Crandall. He'll pick Jacobs up and—"

"No! No police."

"Look, he already knows everything, Teresa," Lark said,

166

dialing the number. "He knows about the green card. He knows about you and Jesus. He knows because a man named Paul Owens was murdered last night, and I had to tell him everything."

"Paul Owens is dead?" Shock vibrated in the words. Teresa's breath came in sharp spurts.

"You knew him?" Lark cradled the receiver after the first ring, before Crandall picked up. Gently, she eased herself down on the edge of the bed. "I'm sorry. I didn't realize."

"I met him in Chiapas. He came to my father's house with Esther once or twice. She was so excited that he was coming here." Teresa's hand groped for Lark's. "Do you believe in heaven?"

Lark shied away from the question. With her aversion to bodies, she didn't feel qualified to answer. "I don't know."

"I do," Teresa said, pulling her hand away.

Not the answer she wanted to hear. "Teresa, do you know a man by the name of Norberto Rincon?"

The girl stiffened. "Why?"

"Because he was asking about you."

Teresa's face paled. "He's a ladino that sells coffee for my father." Teresa gathered her torn skirt, pulling it around her like a blanket. "Did you tell him where I was?"

"No."

The girl doubled over as if in pain. "He's the reason Esther threatened to send me home."

Lark felt as if she'd been sucker-punched. Early on, Teresa had inferred that it was because of the visa. "How so?"

"He works for the PRI."

"I thought your father sympathized with the Zapatistas."

"He does, but the PRI doesn't care about that. They are very pers...How do you say?"

"Persuasive?"

"Sí, that's the word. Señor Rincon forced my father to mix the coffee." Lines of anguish contorted her face. "The whole thing makes me sick."

"What do you mean, mix the coffee?"

"My father grows organic beans, and also some for sun-grown harvest. The organic crop is worth so much more money, but it grows much slower, and there are fewer beans." Teresa's eyes pleaded for Lark to understand. "Norberto Rincon threatened my father. He said, if my father did not sell him some of the sun-grown beans with the tag of the organic, he would destroy our farm."

"So your father complied, and did what Norberto wanted."

"Sí. And Señor Rincon paid him the price for the organic, so, if anyone ever found out, it would look as though my father had cheated him."

"What's the difference in the value, the difference in the price between the types of coffee?"

"The sun-grown beans sell for eighty-five cents a kilo. The organic beans sell for over a dollar." Teresa rubbed her arms against an imaginary chill. "When Señora Mills found out what my father had done, she was so angry. She said selling bad coffee is bad for her business." Teresa cupped her knees to her chest. "If Norberto is in Elk Park, I'm in very bad danger."

Lark stroked the girl's back like she would a baby's. "Don't worry. You're safe here with me."

Teresa fluttered her fingers across her bruised eye and choked out a bitter laugh.

"Right," Lark said, scooting off the end of the bed. "I'm not sure I'd believe me, either."

She left the girl sitting in the bedroom and padded to the kitchen to get some ice for her eye. Bits of information swirled in her head, like pieces of a puzzle waiting to be connected. Find enough of the pieces, find the solution.

She pushed them away. The pieces were Crandall's job, not that he seemed particularly interested in her theories.

She checked the doors, locking both the front and the kitchen, and made sure all the windows were locked up tight. Grabbing a set of towels from the linen closet, she hurried back to the bedroom and handed Teresa the cold compress. "Put this on your eye."

Teresa complied, wincing as she pressed the ice to her bruise.

"I want you to stay here with me. Here's a towel and washcloth. The guest room's this way, down the hall."

Teresa dropped the ice bag and clutched the bedpost with both hands. "No. I don't want to sleep there alone. I want to sleep here, with you."

The king-sized bed proved to be too small for the two of them. Teresa kicked and rolled, moaning in her sleep and consuming three-quarters of the giant bed. Lark felt like a kick-boxer fending off an attack. At five A.M., convinced she'd taken enough abuse, she crawled out from under the covers and crept to the kitchen for coffee.

It was early, but she placed a phone call to Bernie Crandall anyway. Time to unload.

"Bernie, it's Lark. Teresa Cruz showed up."

"When?"

"Two, maybe three o'clock this morning. It seems Jacobs offered to help her, until she didn't come across, then he beat her up. She's asleep in my bed."

"I'll be over in an hour."

Out the kitchen window, the Drummond sputtered to life. The night shift departed. The day shift arrived. The breakfast crew smoked cigarettes outside the back door, while guest room lights blinked on in a random pattern.

Lark sipped her coffee. The one missing piece of the puzzle was the key, the one everything else was constructed around: the ledger. So where had it gone, and who had taken it?

The answer was obvious: one of Crandall's four remaining suspects.

All of them were guests of the Drummond, people with lives that existed elsewhere. When the Migration Alliance ended, provided Crandall let them, they would all go home, leaving Elk Park mourning its dead.

So, thought Lark, suppose I were a guest in town, and I'd murdered two people and stolen something I wanted to hide. Where would I keep it?

Again, the answer was obvious.

In my hotel room.

Aside from the maid, no one uninvited entered a room. A ledger or small ski mask could easily be shoved in a drawer, stuffed into a suitcase, or locked in the room safe with no one ever knowing.

Tomorrow was Tuesday. In two days, the conference would be over, and Esther's killer would walk free.

Lark wondered what it would take to convince Crandall to conduct a search of the guest rooms at the Drummond. A search required a warrant—in this case four—and just cause. Given enough evidence linking a suspect to the crime, the judge might grant him one warrant, but asking for four only proved he was grasping at straws.

She, on the other hand, could gain entry by use of a housekeeping passkey. Shades of Velof. Funny how easy it was to justify bad behavior when it played to your own advantage.

Chapter 17

Her phone rang at five-thirty, while she was in the shower. Shutting off the water, she swaddled herself in a towel and, being careful not to wake Teresa, hurried to the kitchen to answer.

"Lark bunting," cooed her father through the receiver, the childhood endearment sparking a weakness of tears.

"Daddy," she replied in kind. "Did you find out anything?"

"What, no chitchat? No 'Hi, how are you?' Just get down to business, aye? What's happened to your manners?"

His harsh assessment jolted her back to reality, putting tearful sentiment to rest. "I'm sorry, Dad. I'm a little preoccupied."

"You could at least ask about your mother."

"How is Mom?"

"She's fine. Thanks for asking." He chuckled, then she heard him gulp some liquid. Coffee? Orange juice? It was way too early for anything else. "I did unearth some information for you. Seems you were right. Buzz Aldefer is not the birdwatcher he's cracked up to be."

From her father's standpoint, the news was bad. Buzz Aldefer ran a covert operation on foreign soil without proper sanctioning. An Air Force officer working undercover for the CIA, his orders had been issued by a CIA underling by the name of Dean Munger. Aided and abetted by Katherine Saunders, a former grade school chum of Munger's, Buzz had ventured into the heart of Chiapas under the guise of being a birder attached to the Migration Alliance board. His true mission was to gather intelligence for the CIA.

"He's actually Special Ops. The Air Force knows that he's been feeding Munger information for the past seven or eight years."

"And you say Katherine knew also. Did her partner, Paul, know?" Fear of discovery might be enough of a reason for a Special Ops spy to kill someone.

"Munger didn't say. By that point, he was too busy trying to deny everything."

"Did you learn anything more about Katherine?"

"It seems her father, Preston Saunders, defined the term patriot. His birdwatching took him all over the world, and his prestige opened doors to trouble spots the State Department only dreamed of going. They recruited him as early as the 1930s to gather intel for the United States government in Europe."

"Like father, like daughter."

"I wish I could say the same."

A crackle of static on the phone line broke the awkward silence. "I have to go, Dad. Thanks for your help."

"Wait, there's one more thing you should know. Munger thinks there's a chance Aldefer's gone rogue. It seems he's been out of pocket for a while, and Munger thinks he's on the take. Seems he's been spending an inordinate amount of time lately with a known PRI sympathizer by the name of Norberto Rincon."

The image fit: Norberto profited from buying coffee from the Indians for as little as possible, then selling it to Jitters at the top of the market. Not the work of someone who rallied to the cause. Yet he'd spoken softly when stating facts about the plight of the Chiapas Indians, and he seemed genuinely concerned about the plight of the average worker. An incongruity.

As she dressed, she tried assembling everything she knew into separate categories: motives for murder, means, and opportunity. In her mind, the pieces tangled and intermeshed.

The four suspects and two victims had all known each other. They were friends of a sort: partners, lovers, business associates, colleagues.

Means was apparent. The knife used to kill Esther had never been found. The knife used to kill Paul belonged to Lark.

Opportunity was a given. Crandall had already established the fact that nobody had alibis.

Motive was trickier. Possibilities included jealousy, hatred, revenge, self-preservation, and greed. Lark figured money topped the list.

Crandall showed up at six on the nose. Lark caught him up on the latest, then roused Teresa out of bed to answer his questions.

"Where were you at five p.m. the afternoon of August twelfth?"

"Driving." She had taken the Big Thompson Road and ended up in Loveland.

"Can anyone verify that?"

"No."

"What were you arguing with Esther about on the day she died?"

"Money. She owed me money that my father had given to her to keep safe for me."

"How much money?"

"Ten thousand dollars."

Crandall scratched his head. "So, why was she sending you home?"

Teresa looked down at her hands.

"Tell him, Teresa," Lark said. She wondered if the girl's answer would be something other than what she expected.

"My visa had expired. She'd found out that my father was cheating her by mixing shade-grown with sun-grown coffee. Esther said it put her business in jeopardy to let me stay."

Crandall glanced at Lark. "Does INS know about the visa?"

"Not yet. Arquette's working on a solution, but…"

He nodded, asked a few more questions, then stood. "Unfortunately, Teresa, I'm going to have to take you into custody. Under the circumstances, and with the flight risk so high…" He let the sentence dangle.

Teresa cowered on the corner of the living room couch.

"Come on, Bernie. She's just a kid." And possibly a murderer, though the more Lark learned the more convinced she was that Teresa hadn't killed Esther. She knew for a fact Teresa hadn't killed Paul. She couldn't have. And Lark was convinced the two crimes were somehow connected. "Why not take Jacobs into custody and leave Teresa here with me?"

"You willing to take full responsibility for her, Drummond?"

"Sure." Lark prayed her instincts were right.

Crandall hesitated, then turned to Teresa. "Do you understand that if you split, Drummond here goes to jail?"

Teresa looked at Lark. "You have my word of honor. I won't

run away."

"Either you're an idiot, Drummond, or I am." He shrugged on his leather bomber jacket. "I'll be in touch."

Lark sent Teresa back to bed and followed Crandall out the front door. "Hey, Bernie, what are the odds you could get a warrant to search someone's room in the Drummond?" She left the inference open as to whose room she was talking about.

"Nil."

That's what I thought.

Crandall opened the patrol car door. "For what it's worth, we did check out Paul Owens' room and bag his belongings. All we found was a razor and a pile of clothes."

After he left, Lark formulated a plan and checked on Teresa. The girl was sound asleep, exhausted from her ordeal the night before. She'd sleep long enough for Lark to spot-check a few rooms at the Drummond.

Donning a jacket, Lark slipped out the side door and followed the deer path around the back of the Drummond. Below her, Elk Park appeared to stretch as the rays of the sun snaked up the valley and bounced off the asphalt shingles of the buildings. Around her, dew sparkled on pine needles and shimmered on the sleepy faces of the day flowers. The early-morning air smelled of butterscotch pine and biscuits.

Overhead, the birds sang riotously, celebrating the morning, and Lark stopped to listen. Her eyes tracked the darting flight of a yellow-rumped warbler, then a flash of red in the trees overhead rooted her to the spot. Above and to her left, a small bird perched on a branch of a large ponderosa. The red-faced warbler!

The bird preened, ruffling then smoothing its feathers, making sure he was seen. A squirrel chattered nearby, shattering the moment. The bird looked up, then flew away, disappearing among the quaking aspen leaves. Too bad she didn't believe in omens.

The path dead-ended at the edge of the Drummond lawn. Grass, trimmed to one hundred feet out from the hotel walls, maintained a fire buffer mandated by local authority. No trees or bushes were allowed to grow within reach of the building.

No wood to fuel fire. No cover for a surreptitious dash to the back door.

Lark checked to make sure the coast was clear, then sprinted to the back door. If Velof caught her skulking around, her mission was over. Despite the fact that she owned the hotel and had every logical reason to be there, hiding became a necessity.

Muscles tense, senses alert, she scrambled down the back stairs and pushed through the door to the basement. Housekeeping was located in the bowels of the hotel. Pipes, painted gray to match the walls, lined the ceiling. Worn gray and burgundy carpet covered the floor.

Cleaning carts overflowing with toilet paper, tissue, complimentary shampoo and conditioner, towels, and sheets lined up back to back stretched down one side of the hallway. Doorways opened off the other side: the laundry room, the supply room, the office.

Inside the laundry, the rumble of the washers and dryers competed with women's chatter. The air vibrated from the drone of the machines and smelled of fabric softener and bleach. Towels snapped in the air, and were folded on long tables in the center of the room. Two women appeared to dance as they folded sheets.

Lark slipped past without being noticed and hurried toward the main housekeeping office at the end of the hallway. Little more than a cubicle, it housed the housekeeping manual, a desk and computer, and Lydia Escabola, a short, plump Hispanic woman. Lydia managed the housekeeping operation, dishing out cleaning assignments, ordering supplies, and maintaining the schedules. If a guest wanted an extra pillow, more hangers, or clean washcloths, they called Lydia. If a maid fell sick, they called Lydia. If Lark wanted special attention paid to a guest's hotel room, she called Lydia.

"Why Lark, what brings you over here this morning?" asked Lydia, glancing up from the computer screen. She offered a quick, friendly smile.

"I need you to do me a favor."

Lydia's eyes narrowed.

"We have a couple of special guests staying with us. I want

to be sure everything in their rooms stays well stocked."

"I gotcha."

"Can you pull up the room numbers for Jan Halloway, Norberto Rincon, and Katherine Saunders?" Lark already knew Buzz was in room 420.

Lydia's fingers flew over the keys. "Saunders is in 415, Halloway in 312, and Rincon in 314."

Lark jotted the numbers on the palm of her hand. "Who covers those floors?"

"Brenda's on four. Carlene's on third." Lydia looked up from the screen. "Don't worry. I'll make sure they overstock the minibars and leave extra pillows."

"Thanks, Lydia. That'll be a big help." Lark slipped the pen back onto the desk, waved her ink-free hand, and breezed from the room.

Now she had the room numbers. The next step was getting into the rooms. At the far end of the hall, women were loading carts into the elevators. Pushing, shoving, and grunting accompanied the task until eventually all the carts were loaded, and Lark was left alone in the hall. One cart remained, sitting unattended next to the wall.

Lark slunk toward the cart. She found the passkey clipped to the clipboard on top of the cart. Too easy to pilfer. She made a mental note to talk to Velof and Lydia about coming up with a new procedure to make getting hold of one more difficult. A little more rummaging produced a pair of latex gloves.

Now for the hard part. There was no way of knowing who of the targets might still be in their rooms. If she remembered correctly, there was a Migration Alliance breakfast starting in five minutes in the main dining room that Jan, Norberto, and Buzz were scheduled to attend. Katherine was still booked to speak, refusing to allow herself to be replaced, even in light of her partner's murder. If breakfast lasted an hour, that gave Lark sixty-five minutes to check everyone's rooms.

Brenda's cart blocked the elevator exit on the fourth floor. Lark reached to push it aside, but the darn thing weighed a ton. Leaning her shoulder against the metal frame, she gave it a shove, moving it far enough to slip past. Busy cleaning the room across from the service elevator, Brenda never looked up.

Buzz's room was at the far end of the hall on the right, and Katherine's slightly this side on the left. Lark crow-hopped down to room 415, terrified of being caught.

Here goes.

Slipping on the gloves, she tapped on the door, then listened for a rustle, a footstep, anything denoting life. Hearing nothing, Lark tapped again. Still, no answer.

The passkey slipped easily into the lock. The light flashed red, then blinked green. She glanced right, then left, then eased open the door and slipped inside. Clicking the door softly shut behind her, Lark flipped on the light.

The room was in a shambles. Clothes were strewn everywhere, mixed with the covers piled at the foot of the bed on the carpet, draped over the bedside tables. Towels littered the bathroom floor. A pizza box, Pepsi cans, and miniature whiskey bottles overflowed the trash cans.

Stepping over the clutter, Lark wondered if Katherine had thrown a party last night or had just been trying to drown her sorrows. To be charitable, she decided the later.

The rooms on the fourth floor came complete with an oversized desk, two bedside tables, a dresser, TV, and a king-sized bed. Between the door to the hall and the bathroom was a closet with an ironing board and iron. Between the bathroom and the bedroom was an alcove with a microwave, a Mr. Coffee, and a small, well-stocked—or, in Katherine's case, severely depleted—minibar. The door that opened to Paul Owens' adjoining room stood slightly ajar.

Lark started searching in the bathroom, combing Katherine's suite with meticulous care. Cosmetics littered the bathroom counter. Tissues littered the floor. Lark lifted the mattress, checked behind the headboard and in the stored luggage in the closet. If Katherine had the ledger, she'd hidden it well.

Sneaking into the room was easier than sneaking out. Coming in, Lark had the luxury of knowing the room was empty and that no one had seen her enter. Now, she could only press her ear to the door and peer out a peephole broad enough to encompass the door across the hall. Straining her ears and seeing no one, she opened the door and stepped into the hall.

Two people hailed her from the elevator. "Hurry up. We'll hold it for you."

Lark held up her hand. "Oh darn, I forgot something." She waved them off, turning back to Katherine's room. "I'll catch the next one."

The elevator doors banged shut, and Lark sagged against the wall. She could see the headlines in the Elk Park Gazette: "Hotel Proprietor Caught Rifling Guests' Rooms."

Pulling herself together, she scurried down the hall to Buzz's room and repeated the procedure. She'd used up fifteen minutes at Katherine's. At this rate, she wouldn't finish in time.

Buzz's room was immaculate, the exact opposite of Katherine's. In fact, it looked so tidy, Lark wondered if it had even been used. She could have bounced a quarter on the bed, and there were no soiled towels or washcloths in the bathroom.

Well, someone had been in here the night her house had been trashed. She remembered seeing the curtain move.

A thorough search turned up nothing. The ledger wasn't there.

Slipping out into an empty hallway, she tromped down one flight of stairs to the third floor. Carlene's cart was pulled up outside Jan's room, number 312, and the door to Jan's room was open.

She'd just have to start with Norberto's room. She rapped twice. No one answered.

Norberto's room looked unlived in. Not the unused look of Buzz Aldefer's room, but unused as if the occupant felt uncomfortable there. The bed appeared rumpled, indented by someone sleeping on top of the covers rather than under the sheets. A single wet towel hung neatly on a hook on the back of the bathroom door, but the bath mat was untouched and still in place on the edge of the tub. The coffeemaker and the minibar remained untouched.

Norberto's clothes were neatly packed in a small suitcase sitting on top of the desk. Before searching there, Lark checked the dresser drawers, then moved to the bedside tables. One was empty, one contained a set of local White and Yellow Pages.

178

She started to close the drawer, then stopped. Something was sandwiched between the two phone books. Lark grabbed a corner of the White Pages and pulled the book to one side. Underneath, she found what she'd been looking for. A plain, brown, leather-bound ledger.

Flipping open the book, she leafed through the pages. Esther's chicken scrawl leaped off the page, reassuring her it was the real thing. There was page after page of notes, but, after talking with Paul, the numbers made sense. They were Esther's accounting of times and dates and weights, annotated as shipments of coffee made to the United States by Jitters Coffee Company, acronymed JCC. And the numbers were high.

Higher than the 30 percent Jan had claimed Jitters purchased from Norberto. Lark added numbers, rounding up, rounding down. According to her addition, he'd actually sold Jitters over fifty-five thousand bags of coffee last year. Quite a feat, considering Mexico only produced sixty thousand bags of organic coffee. The question was, did Jan know, or was she merely the victim of Norberto's get rich quick scheme?

Spelled out in black and white, the truth of the coffee industry was a tragedy any way you looked at it. Coffee production paid for the livelihood of approximately three million people in Mexico. Modern techniques improved productivity and increased the crop yield but damaged or destroyed the environment. Unfortunately, those who cared the most about the people were the same ones who cared most about what happened to the land, to the bird habitat, to the environment.

Lark's gaze shifted to Norberto's suitcase. She'd started with the bedside drawers and found what she was looking for. But there were still missing pieces to consider.

Crossing to the bag, she carefully lifted the folded clothes out of the bag and set them on the dresser. A clean pair of black jeans, two clean black T-shirts. His underwear was white, plain briefs, Fruit of the Loom.

Nothing.

She repacked the case, taking care to put everything back where she'd found it. Checking one side zipper compartment, she found a toothbrush and toothpaste and miniature bottles of shampoo and conditioner. The other side pocket coughed up the goods. A photograph of Teresa standing in front of a shabby farmhouse wearing a native outfit—and a black mask embroidered with EZLN.

A sudden spurt of harsh laughter erupted from the hallway and jarred her to life. Jan was back. A hand jiggled the door handle.

Shit.

Lark jammed the mask back into the bag and glanced around. There was nowhere to hide. The box the bed rested on was framed in. The windows only opened an inch. There was the shower, but it had a see-through glass door.

"The maid's still in my room. Do you want to go back downstairs with me for a minute?"

Yes.

"No, but you can wait in here."

No.

The drawer where she'd found the ledger stood open. Quickly, she slipped the book back into its hiding place. She had to tell Bernie what she'd found and let him collect the evidence in the proper fashion. Besides, if she got caught inside, she didn't want Norberto to know she'd found everything.

It occurred to her to try standing behind the door when it opened. She'd seen it done in the movies. The door opens, the bad guys enter, the hero slips out. Clichéd, but a plan.

Moving in that direction, she noticed that the adjoining door between Norberto's room and Jan's stood half open. Jan's side was closed tight. A knock might get Carlene's attention.

By the sounds of it, the maid was still vacuuming the room. Lark scurried over and tapped on the door. The vacuum shut off. Lark tapped again.

"Did you hear that?" Jan asked.

Lark tapped again, more urgently this time.

"It sounds like it's coming from inside your room."

The deadbolt on the adjoining door clicked at the same time Norberto inserted his key in the lock. Lark shoved past Carlene, closing the door behind her and flipping the lock.

"Ms. Drummond, what—"

Lark cupped a hand over Carlene's mouth, and alternated between pointing frantically at the door and pressing her finger to her lips. Carlene, wide-eyed and frightened, jiggled her head up and down.

"How strange, Norberto." Jan's voice sounded muffled. Someone tried pushing against the door. "Maybe I should go check out my room?"

Double doo-doo.

Lark scooted around the bed and flattened herself against the wall. Carlene stared wide-eyed at her. Shaking her head, Lark pointed at her eyes, then toward the door.

"Oh. You're still in here."

Carlene faced forward. "Yes."

"Did you hear anything strange coming from my friend's room?"

"No." Carlene glanced at Lark out of the corner of her eye, and Lark prayed Jan wouldn't pick up on the gesture.

"Is something wrong?"

"No." Carlene stayed rooted in place, smiling and nodding like a jack-in-the-box doll.

"How long before you're finished in here?"

"Soon."

"Well, do you mind hurrying up?"

Lark heard movement, a door shut, then Carlene jerked her head sideways and mouthed the word Go.

Quietly, Lark slipped from the room and scooted past Norberto's open door. Bolting down the hall, she yanked open the exit door and bounded down the stairs two at a time. If there was a heaven, this was the time for prayer.

At the second-floor landing, she heard a door open above her and slowed her pace, hugging the wall. As long as she stayed away from the stairwell opening, no one could see her. Besides, the idea that Norberto or Jan had followed her was ridiculous. The door closed again, and no footsteps followed. She breathed a sigh of relief and went on.

Exiting on the first floor, Lark heard the elevator bell ring. The doors opened. Jan stepped off, smiled stiffly, and walked away.

Chapter 18

"Let me get this straight," Crandall said, staring at her from behind his desk. "You broke into Norberto Rincon's room and searched through his belongings."

"For the last time, Bernie, yes. I thought you'd be happy I found something."

"Oh, I'm happy." He stroked his hands through his hair, tipped his head way back, and looked up at the ceiling. "I'm happy to know that Teresa's, okay, and a felon is taking full responsibility for her whereabouts. I was happy to haul Peter Jacobs' butt down here and arrest him for assault. I was happy to hear what your father had to say, and for the update on the coffee wars. But…" He leaned forward again. "I am not at all happy with the stunt you just pulled."

"Why?" She couldn't believe he was angry. "You know you could never have gotten a search warrant. If I hadn't gone in there, you wouldn't have anything."

"I've got zilch now. Nothing I can use, and nothing that ties any of this directly to Esther's or Paul's murders."

Confused, Lark sat back in her chair. "What about the mask?"

"Okay, the mask ties directly to the killing. But we only know it's there because you illegally searched Rincon's room."

"It wasn't a big deal. I was spot-checking housekeeping. I became suspicious and looked around. You now have just cause to go in and collect the evidence."

He snorted like a frustrated bull. "You don't get it, do you? How did you get out of his room?"

"Through the adjoining door into Jan's room."

"Did anyone see you?"

"Carlene, the third-floor maid. What's your point?"

"The maid now becomes a potential witness for the defense. She can testify that you were in Norberto's room under suspicious circumstances, based on the fact you snuck out. Even if I recover the evidence, given the right defense attorney, any judge worth his salt would toss any evidence right out of court on the grounds you might have planted it there."

183

The silence between them stretched. Truth was a hard thing to argue against. "Isn't there anything we can do?"

"We? No! Outside of my finding some hard evidence to prove Rincon or one of the others had a good reason to kill Esther, there's not a damn thing we can do."

"I guess I screwed up."

The regret in her voice must have played through, because Crandall's growl softened. "Look, I'll try bringing him in for questioning. If I say I have reason to believe he's in possession of some items the police are looking for, he may panic and try dumping the stuff. If we can catch him in the act…" He huffed out a breath. "It's a long shot."

"I'm sorry, Bernie." She meant it in more ways than one. The clock was ticking. On Thursday, after her closing speech, the Migration Alliance ended. On Friday, with nothing more than Crandall had to go on, the Alliance members would scatter to the winds, leaving behind only their contact information in the event Crandall wanted to question them.

"Just go home," he said, ignoring her apology. "And stay there. Please."

She'd done as he'd asked. After checking on Teresa, who was eating breakfast, she wandered over to the Drummond Convention Center to sit in on the white paper sessions. Designed as one-hour overviews, the talks covered a variety of bird-related topics and were designed to stimulate, or put you to sleep, depending upon the lecturer and his knowledge or passion for the subject at hand. Lark chose carefully.

The first session covered the aspects of wind and weather. The lecturer, a meteorologist from Cambridge, dutifully explained how high-pressure and low-pressure systems combined to create horrific situations for migrating birds. He told stories of tropical birds, disoriented and lost, arriving in Newfoundland in time for the first winter storm; of birds so tired from being swept up in a hurricane that they died of exhaustion by the thousands on the beaches. Natural weather disasters, while good for the birders, are so bad for the bird populations.

The second session was presented by Katherine Saunders. She looked thinner and older, and her black bob drooped. She wore a pants suit and flats, and for the first time Lark realized how short she was.

"I want to talk to you today about the coffee industry. About its effects on the migratory songbirds of America. For those of you who are unaware, the decline of the Eastern songbirds is significant…"

Lark allowed Katherine's lilting voice to wash over her. She droned on about the farms, the technification of the coffee plantations, the processing plants that polluted the waters - the packaging and sales.

"To stop this decimation, we must become responsible consumers. We must fight to educate the people of our nation. We must sponsor legislation that requires all coffee imports to pass the Food and Commodities agricultural testing limits required for organically grown crops. My friends, this is truly the only way we can hope to insure that the coffee we import is produced in shade and bird-supportive habitat. It is our duty to be responsible consumers."

Testing. The word resonated in Lark's brain, drilled in by the applause of the audience. The speech flowed like political rhetoric—some truth, some skewed perception—lulling the listeners into a point of view. But the words testing triggered an idea.

One hundred bags of coffee sat in the warehouse in Lyons, scheduled for delivery in the morning. Bags of organic coffee from the Cruz farms in Chiapas, Mexico. The same coffee Norberto Rincon sold to Jitters.

Esther must have stopped the coffee deliveries because she realized the coffee Cruz sold her was contaminated with pesticide residue. According to Paul, she claimed to have proof that would blow the lid off the Jitters Coffee operations. The kilo bags, depending on how they were tagged, might or might not provide the link Crandall was looking for. Either way, it was worth a shot.

The police chief was out of the office when Lark called him from home to tell him what she intended to do. She left a message with the desk sergeant to let him know she was headed to the warehouse, and that he should meet her there if he was interested.

"You're going out?" Teresa stood in the doorway in jeans and a peasant blouse. Dark curls cascaded around her shoulders and down her back. Dark eyes appeared vulnerable in the fading light.

"Just for a little while."

"I'm going with you."

A footstep on the front porch caused Lark to whirl around. Jumpy. "It's probably Velof." He'd left her pretty much to her own devices most of the day. She walked toward the door, and heard a clattering of feet. Yanking open the screen, she found no one. A dusty set of prints indicated whoever stood there beat a hasty retreat.

The sun was dropping behind Longs Peak, throwing long shadows across the ground. The parking lot, jammed with cars, separated them from the Drummond. She could hear people laughing in the distance. She sensed someone watching her and glanced up at the fourth-floor windows. A curtain swayed.

Teresa snatched up her sweater. "You can't carry the coffee alone."

Lark's heart crow-hopped. If she had heard the message Lark left Crandall, then the person skulking by the front door might have, also. Damn!

She left another message for Crandall, this one more urgent, then grabbed her keys off the kitchen counter. Like sand through the hourglass, time was running out.

The Commercial Storage warehouses were located in Lyons near the junction of Highway 7 and U.S. 36. The small town, population 1,200, sat at the confluence of the North and South Saint Vrain Canyons, twenty-one miles east of Rocky Mountain National Park at the base of the foothills. What started as a ranching community was now most famous for its annual Canine Festival. Once a crossroads, Lyons was now a budding metropolis, consisting of a main street and several cross streets. Restaurants, bike shops, music shops, art galleries, and antique stores congested the roadways.

It was nearly six when they'd reached the warehouse lot. The sun had dropped behind the mountains and dusk blanketed the valley. Fluorescent lights winked on above the storage areas. Lark glanced in the rearview mirror to make sure she wasn't being followed, then pulled up to the front gate. Black iron fencing encircled the lot. A coded lock box guarded the entrance.

Rolling down the truck window, Lark punched in the number from the file: 12354. Creative security. Keep it simple. That way, the customers will never forget the number and wake up management in the dead of the night, and the criminals will never guess the code is so easy to crack.

Chipe Coffee Company's unit was located around the back side of the buildings, and it was about the size of a two-car garage. Teresa shivered as they rounded the corner and the street disappeared from view.

"It's okay," reassured Lark. "We're alone here."

"That's what I'm afraid of."

Parking the truck, Lark dug in her pocket for the set of keys to the Warbler. There had been two keys that didn't fit any locks at the café or at Esther's house. One or both of them had to fit the padlock on the warehouse door.

The first odd-shaped key didn't work. It didn't even fit in the lock. The second key scraped in halfway and jammed.

"Move it around," Teresa said.

Lark jiggled the key. Slowly, in small increments, it settled into the lock. When it reached its hilt, she turned the key. The padlock popped open. Teresa jumped. Unhooking the lock, she slid back the deadbolt.

The door, made of corrugated metal, rolled up like a garage door. Lark shoved it up out of the way, hooked the lock on the opened door so she wouldn't lose it, and groped for a light switch. A single, long fluorescent tube blinked on.

The building, constructed of a steel frame and wood exterior, contained two small windows blackened with paint at ceiling-level. Several two-by-fours were nailed haphazardly across a hole in one wall, and the concrete floor crumbled in places where water had seeped in and froze.

Piled in the middle of the room were two mounds of bagged

coffee. In one stack, white nylon sacks measuring as long as Teresa and twice as wide held sixty kilos of coffee beans. In the other were smaller bags emblazoned with the Chipe Coffee Company logo.

Coffee was imported raw. In most instances, beans were roasted before they were distributed, but in Chipe's case, some of the smaller specialty stores roasted their own. Talley had indicated there was a shipment ready to go. This had to be it.

She checked the bags. Each one was marked with the type of bean—roasted or raw—the type of coffee, the grade, and the name of the intended recipient. Client names jumped out at her—large chain supermarkets, small cafés, large restaurants—all clamoring for Chipe Coffee.

It was the original mound of coffee that interested Lark the most. The bags shimmered with an iridescent quality some fashion designer would charge millions for. The contents malleable, the bags had shifted until they resembled a pile of pasty bodies stacked four and five deep in places. The necks were clamped shut with huge metal staples and encircled with wire-bearing, stout tags.

The top few tags all read the same: "Cruz Farms. Sold to Chipe Coffee Company." Dated December, they were stamped with the appropriate agricultural mark for organic foods and initialed as received by Esther. Tests run on the coffee would determine whether or not Cruz sold pesticide-laden coffee as organic, but it didn't provide the link to Jitters.

"Teresa?"

At the sound of the male voice, Lark shoved the girl behind her. "What are you doing here? How did you get through the gate?"

"We followed you. The gate was open."

We?

"Jesus?" Teresa cried, clawing Lark's arm to get around her. Norberto Rincon stepped into the light.

"Jesus!" Teresa launched herself into the man's arms.

"Teresa." Rincon spun her in circles, then bent to kiss her. He stopped midway and held her under the light. Pointing to the bruise, he muttered something in Spanish.

"It's nothing." Teresa turned toward Lark suddenly, as though forgetting her manners. "Lark, this is Jesus. Jesus, Lark."

"We've already met." Lark's gaze darted around the warehouse. The two lovers stood between her and the door.

Teresa looked puzzled. "I don't understand."

"He may be Jesus to you, but he was introduced to me as Norberto Rincon."

"What?" Teresa blanched, her coppery skin turning a sickly yellow in the artificial light. She gripped Rincon's arm. "Tell her who you are, Jesus."

"Let me explain it to her," Buzz said Aldefer, stepping around the corner. "I'm with him."

"This is turning into a regular nonbirders birding convention," Lark said, trying to act nonchalant. She grew more uneasy by the minute and prayed the sergeant had given Crandall her message.

"He is not Norberto Rincon," Buzz told Lark.

"I got that picture." She paused, then decided she had nothing to lose by spilling what she knew. "I also know you aren't a birdwatcher," she told Buzz. "You are a spy. You gather intelligence on the Mexican civil war for a man named Dean Munger at the CIA."

"Did your daddy give you that information?"

He'd done his homework on her, just like she'd done her homework on Jan. "Yeah."

"Well, he's got it right, which probably means the gig is up." Buzz's face took on a sad expression, then he shook it off. "Several years back, I met Norberto, the real Norberto, in a bar in San Cristóbal de las Casas. I had information that he was a known PRI supporter, so I struck up a conversation, just to see what kind of information I could get. Turns out he was soused and in need of a friend. He and a partner had come up with this idea to pass off inorganic coffee as organic coffee and pocket the difference. Damned if it didn't work. He used his PRI influence to persuade farmers to go along with him, and sold over four million dollars' worth of bad coffee to Jitters last year. The man's a frigging millionaire."

Lark's anger bubbled up along with her fear. "And you did nothing to stop him."

"Little lady," Buzz said, straightening his bolo tie. "It wasn't my job. My job was to observe and gather intel, and I did my duty."

Duty. The word struck a chord, but the note rang flat somehow. She couldn't hear it clearly or discern what it meant. "You must have been surprised to see Jesus show up in Norberto's place."

"You bet your patootie, darlin'."

She remembered Buzz dropping his glass on the patio. Jesus's reaction, stepping back in the shadows and out of the limelight, made sense now.

"How did you end up coming in Rincon's place?" she asked him.

"Norberto and I come from the same township. I learned he'd been invited to come to Colorado as Jan Halloway's guest, but that he had never actually met her before. We—me and some of my friends—arranged an accident. He is recovering from a broken jaw and a few broken bones right now." His hand caressed Teresa's hair. "I knew my wife was here."

Lark swallowed, touched by his show of affection but afraid of what her next question might bring. She knew she had to ask it anyway. "I found the ledger and a black Zapatista ski mask in your room."

His eyes narrowed. "You were in my room."

She shrugged and made a motion like tap, tap, tap in the air.

"Ahhh, the door. Jan was sooo upset. She tried to fire the maid."

"I know. It didn't work." Lark watched Teresa mold herself against her husband, claiming her rightful position beneath his arm. "You didn't answer my question, Jesus."

"I don't know what you're talking about." His gaze was clear and never wavered. "The mask, I always carry. The ledger, I know nothing about"

Lark believed him. "So who could have planted it there?"

Jan? Propped open, the adjoining room to Jesus' room provided all the access she needed. She could have opened the connecting door at will and slipped the ledger into his room.

Katherine? Velof, in more and more standard practice, had given the coordinators keys to the VIP guest rooms to get them checked-in quickly. The question was, had he given them one per guest or several per room?

Or there was still Buzz to consider. She glanced at the Air Force officer.

"Hey, don't look at me. My job is to—"

"—gather intel," she and Buzz said in unison. "I heard." It took her a minute to realize that her fear had vanished. "Well, now that you're here, you can help us gather some more evidence and haul it out to the truck. Before he died, Paul told me that Esther had proof of Norberto's dealings with Jitters. The inference seemed to be that Jan knew about the coffee."

"Then she might have killed Esther to keep her from spilling the beans," Buzz said. "No pun intended."

Spoken out loud, the thought grew in proportion. "Then," continued Lark, "if she discovered Paul knew there was proof, she would have been forced to kill him, too."

Buzz nodded. "Sort of a Coffeegate."

Lark turned to Teresa. "Teresa, help me check these tags. We're looking for one that's different."

They found it at the bottom of the pile. A tag marked "Jitters Coffee Company." On the back, Esther had written in chicken scrawl: "Hold for pickup."

"By who?" Teresa asked.

"By whom." The woman's voice startled them all.

The light shattered, plunging the room into darkness.

Lark leaped to her feet as the door came down with a clang and the deadbolt slid into place.

"Jan?" Buzz asked. Was he asking because they were just speaking of her or because he thought he'd recognized her voice?

"No," Lark said, matter-of-factly, everything suddenly falling into place. "It's Katherine."

"How did you guess?" With more than two words spoken, the birdlike voice was hard to mistake. Or did she mean how did Lark guess it was she who killed Esther and Paul.

"Your voice gave you away, but the pieces all fit. Paul told me how tirelessly you'd worked to increase the wealth of the Migration Alliance." Rachel's comments about the state of William Tanager's estate came flooding back. Like Katherine's father, he was a renowned ornithologist, and his family was broke. "That's because the family money was running out, wasn't it?"

"Let's face it, even a famous ornithologist is little more than a glorified professor. My father had lived on my grandfather's money, as did his brothers and sister. Suffice it to say, the family resources were stretched thin."

"So you saw an opportunity to make a lot of money and partnered up with Norberto. A little hypocritical, don't you think?"

"The coffee was being sun-grown anyway. Actually, I thought it deliciously ironic that proceeds from its sale were being used to help stamp out its production." She laughed. "Of course, you can imagine my surprise when it wasn't Norberto who showed up for the conference. Luckily, no one was the wiser."

Lark heard the sound of the padlock clicking shut. Fear at being locked inside washed over her. With the windows blackened, no light from outside penetrated the small room, and Lark groped her way closer to the door, the only source of fresh air.

"But why kill Esther Mills?" Buzz asked.

"She had no choice," answered Lark. "Esther had discovered that the Jitters coffee was mixed half and half. Half shade-grown, half sun-grown. And that Norberto was shipping the tainted coffee to the States. Jan Halloway knew nothing about it."

"When Esther told Paul she planned to blow the lid off the Jitters operation, I knew the trail would eventually lead back to me." Katherine didn't move outside the door. "I wore the mask in case someone saw me and surprised her in back of the store. We were about the same size, but I was in much better shape."

Lark's hands touched the metal, found the handle, and yanked up. The door didn't budge.

192

Katherine laughed softly. "You can't get out. I've locked the door."

Panic gripped her; then Lark remembered that Crandall knew where they were. Eventually, he'd come and let them out. She pressed her back to the door frame.

"Killing Paul was more difficult, for a number of reasons," Katherine said. "All of your digging had made him curious. I think he'd begun to realize that I was the one who'd killed Esther. Paul and I had been partners for years. I loved him like a brother. But he carried a torch for Esther, and she was dangerous. She focused too much on the little picture. I'd put a stop to their relationship once, but then he'd rallied to your cause to find her murderer."

Katherine's voice grew faint, then louder again. Lark heard a clanking near the base of the warehouse door.

"I saw him take the walkie-talkie and head into the woods, and I followed him. After he felt he was far enough away from the shelter, he hunkered down near the tree and tried raising someone on the radio. I crept up behind him and hit him with a rock."

"Then slit his throat with my knife."

"Yes." She sounded sad, then perked up. "Though, actually, I thought using your knife was a nice touch."

"Don't you think you've antagonized her enough?" whispered Buzz, grabbing Lark's knee. She jumped, banging her elbow on the metal framing.

"Get up off your knees, Buzz. There's glass from the light all over the place."

"I know. I found some."

A warm, sticky hand grasped her wrist, as he used her for leverage to climb to his feet. She wondered how bad the cut was.

Katherine giggled through the door. "I'm so sorry about this, Buzz."

"I don't know what you're planning to do, Katherine, but why don't you let us out of here, so we can talk about it?" he said. "There's got to be a better solution, and I'm feeling a little woozy from lack of blood."

Lark could hear Teresa whimpering in the background and Jesus whispering sweet endearments to calm her down.

"I can't let you out, Buzz. You forget; I've murdered two people. I imagine they'd put me in jail for life."

Lark nervously worried the end of her braid. "It's only a matter of time before someone comes and lets us out of here, Katherine. There's a coffee delivery scheduled for first thing in the morning, and I left a message with Bernie Crandall's desk sergeant telling him where I was going."

"Then I guess I'd better hurry. Adios, amigos."

Lark felt Buzz tremble beside her, then slump to the ground. Through the door and walls came the sound of a car starting and the smell of exhaust.

Oh my God, thought Lark. Oh my God. Katherine Saunders planned to asphyxiate them.

Chapter 19

For a woman of background and breeding, Katherine Saunders lacked class. Engine exhaust poured in under the door through a large crack on the right side. Lark instantly felt woozy and sick.

"We have to stuff something into the crack and slow down the accumulation of the carbon monoxide." Lark tried to think of what they could use. "Let's empty some of the coffee bags and use the sacks."

"Help me Teresa," said Jesus. "Do what Lark said."

"We need to stay calm," Buzz said, ramming his shoulder against the metal door. "Let's yell for help. If we just sit tight, someone will come."

"Not before we're dead." Lark knew these small towns. On a weekend they rolled the sidewalks up at nine o'clock, on weeknights by eight. Added to it, forested land backed the Commercial Storage lot on one side, while a maze of warehouse buildings buffered the other side from the street. Unless Crandall showed up, no one would find them until morning. And the way things stood, they had about fifteen minutes to live.

"Buzz, you have to get away from the door." Exhaust pooled on the floor at their feet, then rose toward the ceiling on the heat of the fumes. Lark dragged Buzz up from the floor, wrapping his arm around her shoulders, and guiding him toward the back of the small building. Jesus collided with them.

"Sit with Teresa," he commanded, taking over with Buzz and shoving empty coffee sacks into Lark's arms. "What do we do now?"

Lark realized he was looking to her for direction. "You're the guerrilla fighter, Jesus. You tell me."

"I don't know. I've never been in a situation like this one."

Lark heard Teresa praying and scrunched her eyes together. They burned from the fumes, and her head was starting to ache. "Okay, first we need to seal the cracks around the door as best we can."

Together, they shoved the rough burlap into the seam, sealing the crack below the door the best they could and slowing the flow of exhaust into the building.

"I remember seeing two windows, up high, painted black," she said. "If we can break one, maybe one of us can squeeze through. It will at least let some of the exhaust out and some fresh air in."

She could see pinpricks of light penetrating the paint. Jesus leaped into action. Exhaust billowed around them. Lark fought the desire to throw up. "Stay low," she yelled to the others. "It's cold enough, the heated fumes should rise. The air near the floor will stay fresh the longest" She didn't really believe what she'd told them. The exhaust mixed with the air, swirling around them. It was only a matter of time before they succumbed.

Lark patted along the walls, fingers stretched toward the ceiling, searching for the window. The metal framing felt cold to the touch, the boards warm. She tried kicking the wall, to no avail. The structure seemed impenetrable. Just what you want in a security warehouse. If she got out of here, maybe they'd let her do their next commercial.

"I found it," yelled Jesus. His voice sounded hoarse and wheezy. "I can't reach high enough."

"Boost me up." She groped for his hands. "Make a saddle of your hands. Right, like that" She placed her foot in the makeshift stirrup and stood. Her ankle screamed with pain at the exertion. Tears dripped from the corners of her eyes. With one hand she pounded against the glass as she searched for a catch with the other.

Finding a window fitting, she turned the crank, pushing against the glass. Nothing. Damn! "I think the windows are painted shut. We need something to break the glass."

"Boost me," said Jesus, lowering her back to the floor.

Lark formed a stirrup and steadied her hands by leaning her shoulder against the wall. Her head pounded. Jesus shifted his weight, and she winced as the soles of his boots pinched her fingers. She heard his fist pound against the glass, blending with the chug of the car's engine. Teresa began keening, the low moan creating a rhythm with the engine, making a melody of chaos.

The window shattered, and glass rained down on Lark's head. She tucked her chin to her chest and closed her eyes, tensing against the pinpricks of the popcorn shards. Thank heavens for tempered glass.

Jesus jumped down, his breath rattling in his chest. "There's bars on the outside of the windows."

Breaking the window helped a little. It gave the exhaust a place to go, buying them a little more time. It also allowed in some light.

Lark sank to the floor. "Unless Crandall gets here, we're finished."

Teresa's keening increased in rhythm and tempo. Jesus rushed to her side. His gentle Spanish mingled with her cries.

"Would you mind shutting up?" Buzz asked.

His voice, the words. An image of her father at the election podium flashed through her mind, his arms raised. The message: a Drummond never says die.

Maybe she was like her father. Lark pushed herself to her feet. There was a weak link in the building. The hole where the two-by-fours were. Hunched over like a Neanderthal, she moved quickly across the floor. Light from the next storage unit seeped through the bars of the window, helping her find what she was looking for.

"Jesus, come here."

The young man was by her side in seconds. "Tell me what to do."

"We need to tear these boards off. They're covering a hole."

Once the reality of her words sank in, he worked with a fever. Together, they strained against the boards and nails.

"We need something to pry with."

The exhaust filled the room and oozed around them in oily clouds. Anything they did caused them to gulp more of the poisonous air, but not doing anything meant they would die.

"Kick," she ordered. Lark raised her foot and smashed it against the two-by-fours. She found she had better strength standing on her left foot and kicking with her right. Each blow brought an agony of its own, yet a feeling of exhilaration.

On the third kick, the top board gave. She kicked again, and the board splintered beneath her feet. Jesus jerked the board free and used it as a battering ram. In minutes, they'd knocked a hole in the wall large enough for even Buzz to crawl through.

Lark tumbled outside, gulping in the fresh air. Her muscles were weak, she felt sick to her stomach, and a symphony played in her head.

Her mind cleared slightly, and she helped Jesus drag Buzz and Teresa out of the noxious fumes. Buzz babbled incoherently, either succumbing to the poisonous vapors or loss of blood. Teresa shivered and sobbed in the grass. Jesus crumpled to the ground beside her.

Lark rubbed her eyes. She could still hear the symphony.

It blared from the car radio.

"Jesus," whispered Lark. "Katherine is still here."

Of course she was here. She was pumping car exhaust into the warehouse, waiting for the four of them to die.

Leaving the three of them sprawled on the ground, Lark crept along the side of the building and peeked around the corner. Katherine sat in the driver's seat, her head leaned back, her eyes closed. Her hands tapped a rhythm on the steering wheel.

In her compromised state, Lark knew she was no match for Katherine. The woman was strong and in command of her faculties. No, the best bet was to sneak back to the entrance and call Crandall from the pay phone.

Slipping along in the shadows, Lark reached the Commercial Storage office in record time. The pay phone stood in the bright light of a streetlamp, but there wasn't a choice. Lark snatched up the receiver, dialed 911, and told dispatch the problem.

A car door slammed. She heard the scrape of metal against metal. An engine revved, and tires crunched on gravel.

"I have to hang up now." Lark set the receiver down on the metal shelf inside the booth and slipped into the shadows. The gate stood open. You must have to punch in the code a second time to close it. If she didn't do something quickly, Katherine would get away.

The code box was on the other side of the driveway. Darting into the light, Lark scampered across the road. Each footfall caused her head to throb. She punched in the numbers: 12345.

Nothing! Damn. She knew she had the numbers right. Maybe it was the order: 13245.

Nothing.

The sound of the car approaching spurred her to try again: 12354.

The gate arm swung as Katherine turned the corner. She gunned the engine, shooting forward, trying to make the opening. The metal gate clipped the side of her car, pushing her into the gate post, effectively pinning the car in place.

Sirens blared in the distance.

With the news of Katherine's arrest, the Migration Alliance convention ended abruptly. Thursday-morning sessions were canceled, as was Lark's speech scheduled for that afternoon. Attendees milled around like zombies at a zombie festival. Velof stoically endured, helping guests who needed to change their reservations, arranging transportation to the airport, correcting and updating room charges.

Lark watched it all from the confines of the carriage house.

The phone rang, and she answered it.

"Hey, I thought you'd like to know, Buzz and Teresa are both okay," Crandall said.

The night before, they'd all been taken by ambulance to the Boulder Community Hospital. She and Jesus had been treated and released. Buzz and Teresa received a helicopter ride to the nearest hyperbaric chamber. "That's good news."

"How's your head, Drummond?"

"It still hurts."

"And your leg?"

"How do you think? It's back in a cast."

By Monday, badly in need of an outing, Lark hitched a ride with Dorothy and Cecilia to the afternoon EPOCH meeting at Bird Haven.

As Dorothy wheeled the car out of the Drummond parking lot, Cecilia waved to Teresa and Jesus on the porch swing.

"What's going to happen to them?" she asked.

The couple was staying with Lark pending the outcome of an

immigration hearing. "Arquette says they have a chance. Jesus applied for political asylum, and Arquette thinks the judge will grant a hearing."

"I'm glad. They're such sweet young people."

Eric helped Lark up the steps at Bird Haven, settling her into a lawn chair on the patio. He'd stopped by to check on her at least once every day since her trip to the hospital, bringing Chinese food and pizza, and now he situated himself on a bench beside her. Maybe one of these days he'd ask her out on a date.

"Are you okay?" Eric asked. Blue eyes, the color of the sky, searched her face.

Lark nodded, filled with a sudden warmth that made her feel more alive than she had in days. Cecilia, sitting on the other side of her, elbowed Lark in the ribs and winked.

Rachel shoved a glass of iced tea in her hand. "Here you go."

"You've been through quite an ordeal," Andrew said, sitting down opposite and popping a piece of cheese into his mouth. "I've been giving some thought to that climate theory of yours, Lark. I've decided it doesn't fly. It takes too many years for changes to take place. Temperature's one thing, but vegetation doesn't grow overnight."

"What about species that can adapt to a variety of food supplies?" Harry asked, stepping over to join them. "Are you saying they won't change their ranges as global temperatures rise?"

"Some will, some won't," replied Andrew. "I was talking to Lark."

"Did you read that study in the Journal?" persisted Harry.

"Yes. And I'll grant you, it shows that some of the warblers' ranges have pushed north, but there are any number of reasons for that."

"Name a few."

Lark leaned her head back and listened to the men debate. Theories aside, she'd seen the bird. Twice. "You know, I saw the bird—"

"Shhh!" Andrew held up his hand. "Did anyone else hear that?"

"Hear what?" Gertie asked.

"Wi tsi-wi tsi-wi si-wi-wi-wichu," Andrew said, imitating the call.

"How do you do that?" Rachel asked. "That bird sounded just like it. How does he do that?"

"Listen," he said. "Do you hear it?"

Wi tsi-wi tsi-wi si-wi-wi-wichu. The notes, sweet and clear, drifted across the meadow.

"He's somewhere in those trees," Harry said, training a pair of binoculars on a stand of aspen and pine trees growing closer to the creek.

"Where?" Dorothy asked.

Eric looked to Andrew, then Harry. "What is it? A black-throated gray?"

"Maybe."

"No," Andrew blurted, a look of incredulity on his face. "And I don't believe it."

"Believe what?"

"That is the song of the red-faced warbler."

Wood Warblers

Family: Emberizidae
Subfamily: Parulidae

appearance: Referred to as the butterflies of the bird world, warblers are small, often brightly colored birds with slender, pointed bills. Smaller than a sparrow (except for the chat), a warbler's average size is around 5 inches in length. The majority have some yellow in them.

range: Warblers range from Alaska and Canada to northern Argentina, with the designations of many of the individual species offering clues to either their appearance or likely location (for example, the palm warbler is found in Florida palm trees; the Cape May warbler near Cape May, New Jersey; etc).

habitat: Depending on the species, wood warblers live in a variety of habitat, ranging from willow thickets to the tops of the tallest conifer. Some frequent the forest floors, others inhabit the reeds and brushy stream sides, and others live in the twigs and branches of treetops.

song: For most, the warbler's warbling is hardly worthy of the name. They tend to be poor, if somewhat persistent singers. Most have weak voices. There is one exception: the yellow-breasted chat. Blessed with a beautiful, flutelike song, it often sings in the middle of the night.

behaviors: Wood warblers are extremely territorial, defending their turf with thin, wiry songs. They build cup-shaped nests in the fork of a tree branch and lay three to six eggs. Warblers dart and flit, in seemingly perpetual motion, feeding on insects, caterpillars, bark beetles, and similar creatures.

relationship to man: Humanity owes a debt to small birds

such as the warbler, for they are among the world's largest destroyers of insects and related pests. Although warblers account for over 100 species of insect-eating birds, it's become increasingly clear that the ongoing destruction of wintering ground poses a serious danger to the population stability of these birds. The numbers of migrating songbirds in the United States is declining, in large part due to the destruction of habitat in Mexico and Central and South America. In recent years, many of the warblers have been added to the endangered species watch lists, and several hover on the brink of extinction.

Author's Note

The Migratory Bird Conservancy

The Migratory Bird Conservancy is the only program
devoted exclusively to conserving habitat for birds in the
Western Hemisphere. Founded in 1999, the Migratory Bird
Conservancy was created by birding businesses who make
binoculars, feeders, and other equipment, and who package and
sell seed and other wild bird foods. Their goal—to protect
important bird habitats in North and South America.

For every $1 contributed to the Migratory Bird Conservancy,
more than $4 in on-the-ground habitat conservation is
accomplished through federal funds and matching grants. A
steering committee makes funding recommendations to the
foundation, and administrative costs are paid solely by interest
generated by the fund, or special donation. Which means every
dollar donated goes to help conserve habitat.

Take Bosque del Apache National Wildlife Refuge, located
in Socorro, New Mexico. It is one of the hottest birding and
wildlife-watching sites in North America. Each fall, tens of
thousands of snow geese, sandhill cranes, and dozens of other
species stop at this site. Bosque del Apache is an important
habitat link for migratory birds that nest in the U.S. and Canada
and travel to Mexico and southern points for the winter. And, in
addition to the birds, Bosque del Apache attracts more than
17,000 annual visitors.

However, a silent invader threatens this critical refuge.
Creeping in from the edges is saltcedar, an invasive, exotic tree
that destroys the wildlife values of western wetlands. Saltcedar
can be controlled, but it's costly and time consuming. With the
award from the Migratory Bird Conservancy, two hundred acres
of valuable wetlands will be restored.

To date, the Migratory Bird Conservancy has helped protect
and improve habitats in famous birding sites such as Cape May,
New Jersey, New River State Park in North Carolina, and
Bosque del Apache National Wildlife Refuge. But the need is

great, and your participation is needed. By making a tax-deductible contribution to the Migratory Bird Conservancy today, you can help keep the future bright for our birds!

Benefits of Contributing to the Migratory Bird Conservancy:
• tax-deductible contributions
• no administrative costs—every penny protects bird habitat!
• minimum 4:1 leverage for every $1 contributed

Visit the Migratory Bird Conservancy Website at www.conservebirds.org for more information! And please support the companies listed on the Website that support the Migratory Bird Conservancy. Every time you purchase their products, you support bird conservation.

Acknowledgments

Death of a Songbird posed a different set of challenges than my first book, so a special thank-you needs to go to all the people who kept me honest.

To Janet Grill, a fellow writer, dear friend, and the best plotting partner a girl ever had; Janet Chapman, who dragged me off to several writing conferences and forced me to dig deeper; and Anne McHugh, who threw the party that helped put me on the local bestseller list—thank you. To the RMFW critique group that faithfully meets twice a month at Marie Callender's: Gwen Schuster Haynes, Suzanne Proulx, Louise Woodward, Janice Ford, Diane West, Janene McCrillis, Mary McPhee, Bob Strange, and David Jones; the MWA support group that meets the third Wednesday: Georgeanne and Steve Nelson, Barb and Leslie Stephens, Stephanie and John Kane, Christine Jorgensen, and Carol Caverley; and Liz Hill, Alice Kober, and Peggy Waide—you kept me smiling while you worked my tush off.

I also would like to acknowledge Scott Roederer, Rhonda Woodward, Father Tom, Margaret Harmon and all the other birders who attended the American Birding Association and Colorado Field Ornithologists conventions in Colorado. Your patience in helping me learn new skills, spot new birds, and your invaluable suggestions were greatly appreciated.

And, finally, a special thanks to my agent Peter Rubie for his unwavering support; Georgie Nelson, for her dynamite web design; and my family, for putting up with late dinners.

Printed in Great Britain
by Amazon